water

worlds between heaven & earth

1

Water—
a covenant of life
both miracle and marvel
shining clear
emerging
from the grounds of rock
or meadow,
sand or earth
in rapid flow
toward the sea
from spring to brook,
then river-stream,
moved by its inner law.

2

As clouds too
as breath of air
fine in the worlds above,
as veil of fog, as silverfrost,
as snow, as hail

and as wall of rain
attiring bush and field
nursing
so new spring green
may grow to harvest
life upholding.

3

Silence is around
each creature
going down to water
bowing low
and drinking
knowing of no hunt.
Like paradise—
the antelope stands
near the lions.
Down at the water
there
life is more near
than death.

4

This planet earth
speaks to us
when floods come over
man and land.
A breath, a gorge,
a cry,
black substance now
fright, horrorforce
in gushing
downward
all.

5

The water seems
a part of what
the Lord speaks unto us.
It is commandment too,
and confidence and trust.
A well of life

and mercy too—
a punishment
for disconcern
when we defy its laws
that teaches life.

6

Bowing low the head
down at the river
when
the sun is rising
from the night,
raising in the hand
a bowl of water
asking the benediction
for self and world,
from what is known
of the Divine within
we ask for peace.

BRIGITTE SMITH

water

worlds between heaven & earth

photographs by
ART WOLFE

text by
MICHELLE A. GILDERS
& CLAUS BIEGERT

STEWART, TABORI & CHANG
NEW YORK

water

worlds between heaven & earth

by MICHELLE A. GILDERS

If you could capture the essence of life, what would it look like? A rainbow filled with brilliant colors? A waterfall in constant motion? A wave thundering to shore until the very beach shudders at its power? And if you could capture the essence of fluid thought and imagination, would it look the same?

Water is more than habitat, it is life. It suffuses our planet, just as it suffuses our bodies. Water has shaped our Earth, our evolution, our physiology, our societies, our cultures, and our religions. The lack of water is synonymous with death, its abundance with prosperity. It is through the constant recycling of water, from the atmosphere to the oceans, from rivers and lakes to underground aquifers, and from glacial ice to the first flurries of snow, that life has taken its cue and revealed an immense variety of forms. To the ancients, our world consisted of four elements: earth, air, fire, and water. But it was the last that dominated, for water shapes Earth, is carried on the wind, and extinguishes flame.

I have always had a fascination with water. Perhaps it arises from growing up in an island nation where no point of land is more than 75 miles from the sea, and a preoccupation with the vagaries of the weather has become a national characteristic. Or perhaps it is my Anglo-Irish blood that delights in vistas where land and cloud merge into a single entity, and where ever-present rainfall heralds a "soft day." Or it could be my current residence in Western Canada, where long, glacially carved fjords and valleys incise the land, whales and sea lions frolic offshore, and ample rainfall feeds waterfalls, lakes, and moss-covered forests. All I know is that I am drawn to places with a connection to water, whether lapping against the shore, constrained by riverbanks, falling from dark and brooding clouds, or steeled in snow and ice.

Every species on Earth is completely dependent on water, from the 98-foot-tall tree that relies on capillarity to raise water from its roots to its leaves, to the aquatic insects that use the surface tension of a pond to skim across the water's surface, to the spadefoot toad that spends eleven months of the year dormant beneath desert sands, to the myriad marine creatures whose forms are shaped by the buoyant, salt-rich waters of the oceans.

Water covers more than 71 percent of Earth, and 97.95 percent of that water is contained within oceans and seas. I am fortunate to have seen many of these vast reservoirs for myself: the Arctic Ocean, the Bering and Chukchi seas, the North and South Pacific, the Scotia Sea, the Atlantic, the North Sea and the Irish Sea, the English Channel and the Mediterranean, the Gulf of Alaska and the Caribbean, the Sea of Cortez and the Gulf of Mexico, the Straits of Juan de Fuca and the Straits of Magellan. I've crossed the Drake Passage and the Bering Straits. I've traveled the Inside Passage and the Beagle Channel. What never ceases to amaze me is how a transparent substance like water can take on so many different guises.

Water reflects the things around it. It takes sunlight and clouds, wind and rain, and turns itself into something different. Alchemists have long searched for a universal substance, something that can transform the mundane into the desirable, the worthless into the priceless. That substance may yet prove to be water.

In the turbulent, productive waters of the South Atlantic, gray waters tip over into white-caps under a never-ending wind. Close to towering islands subsumed under glacial ice, the water turns emerald, clouded with glacial flour. Beneath icebergs, the depths become a shimmering green, and under a rare blue sky, the water glistens with stars, reflecting mountains of ice with perfect clarity; mirror images of gigantic peaks. Here, on the fringes of a frozen world—the world that Captain Cook called "a country doomed by nature to lie buried under everlasting ice and snow"—I watched penguins flying through water, hundreds of thousands of shearwaters and albatrosses flock over schools of fish, and orca chase humpback whales between floes of ice.

In the clear, warm waters of the Sea of Cortez, I have danced with California sea lions, weaving back and forth with them while angel fish, sergeant-major fish, and box fish swam below. In the emerald and sapphire waters of the South Pacific, I have snorkeled with stingrays and mantas over golden sand and coral reefs on the sunken slopes of volcanoes. I have watched polar bears jump from ice floe to ice floe in a northern ocean, their creamy coats contrasting with the dirty white of summer ice, and seen bowhead whales escorted by bone-white belugas swim through open leads.

The water looks different in every ocean. It is warm and cold, windswept and becalmed, blue, gray, green, white, black, transparent and opaque, impenetrable and inviting. It is in waters like these that life first blossomed and the first people sought to explain their creation.

Throughout human history, water has evoked fear and wonder. Storms and floods were attributed to dark and vengeful gods, while seasonal rains that fed crops and lakes were the gifts of more compassionate deities. Water healed and purified. Water reflected all that was around it, and under favorable circumstance, water droplets lit by an emerging sun could lead the lucky to a pot of gold.

To the ancients, Earth itself was born out of water. The Cherokee of North America tell of a time when water covered Earth and all living things lived above the rainbow. It was crowded where the animals lived, so they sent Water Beetle down into the water to see what he could find. Water Beetle dived to the bottom of the ocean and brought some soft mud to the surface. The mud spread out in four directions and formed a vast island that floated on the water. This was Earth. When the mud had dried, all of the living things descended from the sky and lived on the dry land.

Some tales of the oceans and creation myths are universal; the same themes wind their way through cultures like a river that links far-flung nations to a common source. In Mesopotamian legend, the gods created humans out of clay to act as their slaves. Ultimately they grew displeased with their creation, and decided to destroy the world with a flood. It was Enki, the god of water (familiar to us today as the astrological figure Capricorn), who warned a man called Ziusudra of the coming cataclysm. Ziusudra built a huge vessel and rode out the flood until the waters subsided. Judeo-Christians later adopted this myth, and Ziusudra became Noah.

Do the oceans simply invoke similar tales out of the human imagination, or is the link something deeper, something suggestive of a memory shared by people as geographically separate as the Sumerians and the Incas? Some geologists believe that the North American ice cap underwent a major collapse and melted almost 12,000 years ago, resulting in an extremely rapid rise in the world's sea level. Such an event would have affected coastal peoples around the world, and could have been the basis for a universal story of a great flood.

Humans are a terrestrial species, confined to island continents surrounded by an all-encompassing sea. And while water may sustain our bodies in the most basic sense, it also does something far more substantive: it stimulates us. Water brings out the explorer in us; we demand to know what lies just beyond the horizon. It awakens the scientist in us who demands to know what makes the currents move and the tides rise and fall. It arouses the biologist in us who dives below the surface in search of barely imagined creatures. And it brings out the poet and the philosopher in us who see the whole world reflected in water, from the Sun and the Moon to our own searching faces.

Water as metaphor fills our language and our thoughts. In Shakespeare's words, "Smooth runs the water where the brook is deep." The mirror a stone cannot crack. The stuff of life. Forever changing and forever remaining the same. The author H. E. Bates wrote: "Water has some kind of powerful mystery about it. Still waters, moving waters, dark waters; the words themselves have a mysterious, almost dying fall."

There is a circularity in the flow of water around our planet, an unending motion fed by the heat of the Sun. There is an inherent mystery entrenched in this cycle, the mystery of constancy linked with change, and transformation with unity. It began with the birth of our planet, and it will end with the death of our life-fostering star.

Earth was formed out of interstellar dust and debris that collected around the Sun 4.6 billion years ago. Material continued to collide and amass until 3.8 billion years ago. As the planet cooled, water escaped from Earth's minerals and condensed on the surface, forming the great oceans that dominate our misleadingly named home. This water was imbued with energy from the Sun. It is that energy—combined with the gravitational attraction between Earth, the Moon, and the Sun—that imparts such dynamic characteristics to water. It is almost synonymous with movement in our minds: flowing, rising, sinking, plunging, crashing, running, gushing, roaring water.

It is a deceptively unique substance, and its chemical simplicity belies its complex nature. Water was first synthesized in 1781, and the "primal element" was revealed as a compound. It consists of associations of two atoms of hydrogen and one atom of oxygen, covalently bonded to form a three-dimensional molecule, H_2O. Hydrogen bonds also form between the hydrogen atoms of one molecule and the adjacent oxygen atoms of another molecule, resulting in a variety of latticelike structures that are at the heart of water's special nature.

When water occurs as a vapor, the water molecules are essentially independent, and hydrogen bonds between molecules are uncommon. As a liquid, hydrogen bonds become frequent, resulting in a short-range lattice structure that gives water its relatively high viscosity, its high surface tension and its high boiling point. Below 32° Fahrenheit, water displays more unique characteristics: it forms an ordered, regular lattice that, unlike the solid forms of most other substances, is less dense than its liquid. The result is that solid water—ice—floats. If this were not the case, rivers and streams would freeze from the bottom up, the survival of freshwater organisms during long winters would be in doubt, and we would not be able to delight at the sight of a towering iceberg, sculpted by wind and water into the shape of a natural cathedral or dramatic archway.

It is the hydrological cycle that links water to the biosphere. Heat initiates and maintains the cycle, but gravity keeps it moving. Solar radiation is absorbed by the oceans, and water molecules evaporate into the atmosphere. Since warm air can hold more moisture than cold air, rainfall is highly dependent on temperature. If, for example, a warm, moist air mass is pushed up against a mountain range, the air cools and the moisture is released as rain or snow. This precipitation may run directly into a river or lake, or be intercepted by vegetation or absorbed into the soil; some will evaporate back into the atmosphere, while a portion may seep into the ground, reaching underground aquifers. Eventually, however, gravity wins out, and water seeks out its lowest level and returns to the sea, only to begin the cycle once again.

Hydrologists talk of residence times for water, that is, the amount of time it takes to completely replace the water at each stage of the cycle. The oceans have a residence time of 37,000 years. Lakes have residence times that range from months to years, rivers generally replace their water in a matter of weeks, while the atmosphere replaces its water content in about ten days. We have come a long way since the days of Plato and Aristotle, when great passageways were believed to channel water through the center of Earth so that mountain springs could be replenished by the sea.

Ever since the earliest explorers took to the rivers, lakes, and oceans, sailors have learned from the water. Long before scientists documented, analyzed, and gave names to the phenomena they witnessed, seafarers and rivergoers knew the practical implications of tides, currents, eddies, and waves.

Earth is under the influence of celestial objects, just as it was born from them. The earliest of peoples knew this, and they crafted their myths and legends to give great powers to the objects that were beyond their reach. Human curiosity is matched only by a desire to tell stories.

The Moon was long known to hold power over water. Among the Tlingit of southeast Alaska, the mischievous and cunning Raven (the immortal trickster who embodies more human qualities than avian ones) battled the Old Woman (Moon) who was Mistress of the Tides. After a long battle in which the Old Woman was prodded unmercifully with the spines of sea urchins, Raven won the battle and laid claim to the land revealed at low tide, giving homes and sustenance to intertidal creatures.

It was not until Sir Isaac Newton developed his fundamental laws of mechanics that the gravitational effect of the

Moon, augmented by the Sun, gained universal acceptance. Today, we may forget that the two high tides our coastlines experience each day owe their passage to such a remote but highly visible neighbor; however, intertidal communities and coastal ecosystems owe their evolution and continued survival to such predictable forces.

While the Age of Science did not begin revealing the reasons behind nature's actions until men like Copernicus, Newton, Galileo, and Kepler delved into the visible manifestations of the laws of physics, explorers of bygone ages were taking to the seas with only the knowledge of their forebears to guide them; but that knowledge would allow them to journey around the world.

We do not know when the first people took to the water, or what their motivation may have been for leaving the security of the land; we can only imagine that they would have been as curious as we are today. Perhaps they wanted to know where the seabirds went, or where the strange objects were from that washed up on their shores. Perhaps they simply wanted to catch the fish they could see jumping beyond the surf.

Archaeological studies suggest that people first began fishing around 20,000 BC. The Greeks were trading throughout the Aegean Sea in 10,000 BC. By 3,000 BC, a thousand years after the wheel had been invented, ports were a crucial part of trade across the Mediterranean.

But when did the first tentative voyage take place? Surely long before the Greeks. When did people first realize that they could take advantage of floating logs to fashion canoes, or that animal skins could be stretched over bones or wooden shafts to make a kayak, or that the reeds they watched floating downstream could be tied together to make a raft?

Aboriginal Australians arrived on the remote continent more than 40,000 years ago, and even though sea levels were far lower than today, they would still have had to cross more than 50 miles of open water to reach the new land mass. Did they swim, or did they fashion vessels to assist in their journey?

The world's climate remained cold long after the maximum period of glaciation in 18,000 BC, but by 13,000 BC, the warming trend was well underway, and the water locked up in the great ice sheets was gradually released, swelling the oceans and raising sea levels. During maximum glaciation, the sea level was 400 feet below today's level. Between 15,000 and 10,500 BC, the oceans rose 66 feet. After another thousand years, sea levels rose a dramatic 79 feet; another 92-foot rise occurred after 8,500 BC. The environment was transformed from cold continental to warm and coastal.

Inevitably, some people took advantage of the shallow continental shelves and tidal estuaries that rising sea levels created. The end of a major glacial period allowed *Homo sapiens sapiens* to spread around the globe. Rising temperatures flooded land and separated islands and continents. Among other species, isolation can lead to an accumulation of genetic changes, giving rise to new characteristics and sometimes new species. Among humans, separation and isolation foster cultural identity. The oceans were the unknowing and silent accomplices in an explosion of human diversity.

However, the oceans did not isolate entirely. Curiosity and exploration became survival skills that were propagated through maritime societies as effectively as any successful gene. Just as hunters learn the behavior of their prey, seafarers became oceanographers long before the science of oceanography existed.

The Polynesians, in particular, became adept seafarers. They reached New Caledonia in 2,550 BC, Melanesia in 2,000 BC, Samoa in 1,800 BC, Vanuatu around 900 BC, Tahiti in AD 600, and New Zealand in AD 1000. Other voyagers made similarly impressive journeys, although not all can be verified. The Phoenicians, who dominated seafaring in Europe from 1,000 to 250 BC, may have rounded the Cape of Good Hope to reach the Indian Ocean; some believe they even crossed the Atlantic. Irish legends tell of St. Brendan's voyage to the New World in AD 550, in a simple curragh made from animal skins. The Vikings may have set foot in North America in AD 1003. A Welsh prince supposedly sailed to Florida in 1170. And an Arab legend tells of the Muslim King Abubakari of Mali who sailed to South America and met the Incas in 1311.

Did these voyages take place? Some surely did, others probably did not. How many voyages were begun but failed, lost in the abyss after a devastating storm or mired forever in an unrelenting calm? For all the successes that history has recorded, there must have been countless more that were reclaimed by the sea, arrested by the waves and wind for having the arrogance to explore. But curiosity cannot be denied, just as the sea cannot be contained.

The early explorers may have been blessed more with luck than ability, but in a surprisingly short period of time, seafarers were using the stars to navigate, keeping course by the Sun, interpreting ocean swells, marking the positions of clouds standing over islands, observing the behavior of birds and other marine creatures, and following currents along invisible highways.

Wind-driven currents dominate the oceans, aiding in this migration of humanity. The wind drives a surface layer of about 328 feet of water, while the ocean in turn exchanges heat with the atmosphere, establishing atmospheric circulation patterns.

A series of large gyres—rotating currents that pirouette and twirl across the sea—encompasses the oceans in predictable cycles. The currents interconnect like the cogs in a machine: the Pacific South equatorial current links with the South Pacific current, the Kuroshio with the North Pacific and then the California currents, and the Gulf Stream with the North Atlantic and the Norwegian currents. Currents merge and separate, urged on by the winds that the oceans themselves help to generate.

Sailors gave other names to the places that helped or hindered their passage. Despite its treacherous nature, the Black Sea was originally called "The Hospitable" by the Greeks because it was believed unwise to give a force of nature a derogatory name. It was the Turks who renamed the dark and foreboding sea Black. The Cape of Good Hope was once the "Cape of Storms" before being renamed by the King of Portugal because its original name discouraged vessels. The Horse Latitudes were supposedly named because sailing ships carrying horses to America would throw their unfortunate cargo overboard when becalmed, while the Pacific Ocean was named by Magellan during his voyage around the world because it offered such a respite from the storms he and his crew had endured in the Atlantic. Given the unforgiving nature of storms in the Pacific, perhaps Magellan was simply following in Greek tradition.

Below the currents that move ships, life rises and descends. Life exists even where sunlight does not penetrate. There the cycle of life is maintained by the hydrogen sulfide spewed out by the molten heat of Earth.

The oceans contain an estimated 10 million species, although only 295,000 have been identified; 90 percent of Earth's biomass resides in the sea. The so-called neritic zone encompasses the first 656 feet of the ocean, out to the continental shelf, with the epipelagic zone covering the first 656 feet of oceanic water. Here whales and dolphins live in that boundary between water and air, shaped by the former but as dependent as any other mammal on the latter. Cyanobacteria, ancient forms of life that emerged 3.3 billion years ago, almost as the first oceans cooled, travel where the currents take them, converting the sun's energy and providing the foundation for the oceanic food web. Feeding on the phytoplankton are other plankton, which feed the fish, which feed other fish, which feed the mammals and the birds. The marine food chain intertwines around its inhabitants, sometimes the predator and sometimes the prey.

Below the neritic zone is the bathyal zone, which reaches to 13,123 feet, and below that is the abyssal zone. Then there are the great marine trenches, plummeting to more than 26,247 feet (the Marianas Trench is the deepest point on Earth at 36,161 feet). It is startling to think that 92 percent of the ocean, roughly two-thirds of the globe, lies below 656 feet. Although light can dimly penetrate to 1,739 feet, most of the ocean is dark, cold, and under extreme pressure. With no light penetrating to the sea floor, the organisms that inhabit this place rely on the continuous rain of organic debris from above, scavenging death to maintain life. It is a world as alien to us as anything we could hope to discover in space. We may have mapped the upper, dry world, but we have barely dipped our feet into the abyss.

Water presents life with an almost perfect habitat. Its high specific heat—the ability to absorb or lose a large amount of heat before significantly changing temperature—provides aquatic organisms with an environment that is far milder than comparable terrestrial systems; even at the poles, life can flourish beneath the ice, while temperatures above may be -49° Fahrenheit or colder.

Water's high density gives the largest and smallest of living things complete support, and special adaptations like the swim bladder allow fish to rise or fall in the water column. Water is also one of the best known solvents. Ever since the first oceans formed and the first rivers began to flow, water has carved into the land, dissolved rock, and absorbed gases. Today, sea water contains eighty-four of Earth's one hundred three elements, including nitrogen, phosphorus, silicon, and iron. If water were not such a good solvent, the nutrients essential for life may have remained forever unavailable.

However, the oceans are not uniform. Since water is denser and more viscous than air, the mixing and diffusion of substances occurs much more slowly. The result is that ocean waters may become locally deficient in oxygen, phosphorus, or other essential elements limiting the distribution of life; in many ways the deep, open ocean can be considered a desert.

The ocean also tends to "lock up" nutrients in its sediments, taking them out of circulation until undersea storms stir up the muck. Unending thermohaline currents, fed by cold water that sinks to the bottom at the poles, move slowly across the sea floor. However, the sea floor is not level, and these currents are blocked by vast submarine mountain ranges, as well as continental land masses. When the thermohaline currents meet such an obstacle, the bottom water is forced upward in a mechanism known as upwelling. Those regions that experience upwelling, such as the west coasts of North and South America, West Africa, and the Arabian Sea, are incredibly productive. They make up only 0.1 percent of Earth's oceans, but they contribute more than half of the world's fish catch.

The oceans are the start and the end of the hydrological cycle that envelops Earth. The rain, snow, sleet, and hail experienced on land usually have their beginnings at sea, no matter how far inland. Only about 11 percent of all precipitation results from moisture evaporated by continental air masses; almost 90 percent is derived from air masses that picked up their moisture over the sea.

What does water look like when it is released from the confines of a marine basin? With the hydrogen bonds between molecules broken by heat, water becomes something ephemeral. It moves invisibly through the air until a cooling occurs that reconnects water molecule with water molecule. When the relative humidity of the air exceeds 100 percent, invisible water is revealed in the form of a cloud.

Clouds are the fugitive, fleeting manifestations of water, temporary mists between ocean and land. "The sky too belongs to the Landscape," wrote Luke Howard, the nineteenth-century father of British meteorology. "The ocean of air in which we live and move, in which the bolt of heaven is forged, and the fructifying rain condensed, can never be to the zealous Naturalist a subject of tame and unfeeling contemplation."

We speak of having our head in the clouds when daydreaming, and of being on Cloud Nine when happy. Every cloud has a silver lining. Clouds are the breath of gods, the pillows of angels, and the gossamer trails of divine chariots. Who can forget Wordsworth's poignant poem of the imagination: "I wandered lonely as a cloud"?

Clouds combine the power of the ocean and wind. At times intangible, sometimes subtle traces in the upper reaches of the atmosphere, at others bearing the intensity of a cyclone and the head of a storm. The names given to cloud formations conjure up wonderful images: cirrus, "a lock of hair"; cumulus, "stacked"; stratus, "layered"; and nimbostratus for the gray, brooding clouds that bring "widespread rain."

Clouds lie across the land, folding into contours and valleys. They blend with it, sometimes hiding the land from view, sometimes revealing small pieces of it as they move on soft breathes of wind. They are drawn to islands amidst the great seas that gave them substance, shrouding volcanic peaks as though hiding a secret from prying eyes. Clouds descend to caress the tops of trees, leaving dripping moisture in the wake of mist and fog. Amid equatorial rain forests, moisture brought from the ocean is supplemented by water evaporated from the dense, green growth. Rain forests make rain, and clouds and leaves exchange water between them.

Before rain can fall, water molecules must first condense around small atmospheric particles called condensation nuclei. These tiny particles may be natural, like volcanic dust, or of artificial origin such as the products of industrial combustion. Water condenses around these nuclei to form a cloud droplet. Combine one million cloud droplets and you have a typical drop of rain. As droplets grow, they eventually gain sufficient mass to fall to the ground. In the tropics, the cloud droplets remain liquid throughout this process. In most other areas, though, before it can rain, these droplets must first turn to ice.

It was the German meteorologist and geophysicist Alfred Lothar Wegener who developed the theory that raindrops actually come from ice crystals. In 1911, Wegener realized that clouds high in the atmosphere would be cold enough to form ice and that as the crystals grew in size, they would eventually fall, warming on their descent and melting to form raindrops.

Snowflakes are the delicate emissaries of winter. They fall to the ground in an almost endless array of shapes: plates, stars, columns, needles, spatial dendrites, capped columns, and irregular crystals. Individually, snowflakes are clusters of these minute crystalline shapes; collectively, they are the brusque attendants of frigid temperatures and a low, heatless sun.

Almost a quarter of Earth's land area may be blanketed by snow during the year. It falls in soft layers that silently turn forests white, hanging heavily on the boughs of trees and bending others low. It smothers grassland and tundra, muting the landscape and burying valleys beneath a brilliant but blinding glare.

Carried on the leading edge of a storm, delicate snowflakes become something more deadly, an unthinking and uncaring sort of fatal beauty that wraps the unwary in icy arms. The ice crystals blown by the wind become a lethal weapon at the cold heart of which is a blizzard. Take a blizzard to its most extreme point, and you have a white-out. A white-out is like stepping into oblivion. There is no up and down, no left or right, no near or far. You lose yourself in it so completely that the world itself disappears. There is no middle ground in the midst of a white-out; either you make it to the other side or you don't.

I love the freshness that a covering of white gives to the land. I enjoy the sensation of stepping on untouched snow at twenty below freezing and listening to the crystals crack underfoot, of breathing in frigid air and watching my own exhalation materialize before me.

There is a quiet solitude contained in winter. Thundering waterfalls are frozen, locked in sheets of ice that cascade down a rock face, the appearance of movement arrested by plummeting temperatures. Lakes lie hidden beneath thick ice, their life slowed but not stopped. Rivers fight longer against the constraining hand of ice, but eventually they too can succumb to the transformation from liquid to solid. Shallow water bodies may freeze to the bottom, killing fish that have strayed there. Deeper lakes and rivers provide vital overwintering habitat for these fish, a point not missed by hardy fishermen who drive their trucks onto frozen lakes and bore holes through the thick ice to reach the water below.

Some animals are biologically programmed to avoid winter's harsh conditions through hibernation; others avoid the snows completely by migrating south. For those that remain active—wolf, caribou, moose, lynx, snowshoe hare—winter is about day-to-day survival. Deep winter snows can cull a herd more efficiently than any hunter. To the young, the old, the weak, the sick, winter may be beyond endurance. Such is the balance of nature. Some years may, to our narrow vision, seem extreme, but over time there is a cycle that unites the predator and prey, the grazer and its forage, the fisher and its catch. Life and death are mediated by nature without emotion.

Winter passes with a seasonal certainty. It flows from autumn and transforms into spring. As temperatures warm and the snows melt, rushing forth to join other water released from winter's tight grip, life emerges. New growth sprouts from the tips of branches, green leaves unfurl, sap begins to flow, and energies are channeled towards the creation of new life. Animals seek out others of their own kind. Winter's quiet becomes spring chaotic. In some places, however, winter does not leave. It hangs on in the form of cascading glaciers tumbling down the sides of mountains, or in the form of ice caps permanently fixed to towering peaks, or in the shadows along valley walls hidden from the Sun.

The land owes much to the mantle of ice that has come and gone over millennia. Water turned solid gives rise to the most powerful, mightiest rivers on Earth. These rivers of ice scour the land, defeating even the hardest of rocks. The nineteenth-century Swiss geologist Louis Agassiz called glaciers "God's great plough." They carve vast trenches as they advance and retreat, moving millions of tons of material and leaving behind a barren lunar landscape that is only gradually reclaimed by plants.

Today, glaciers cover slightly more than 10 percent of the world's land and hold 75 percent of the world's fresh water. In the past they shaped our mountains and valleys, the course of rivers and the lie of lakes.

Glaciers have their beginning in snow that survives the passage of winter. This "firn" accumulates in mountain hollows and, with the weight of additional snowfall, gradually transforms into glacier ice. The ice erodes into the surrounding rock, gradually deepening the hollow to form a cirque, and eventually the developing glacier pushes out of its confines and descends down into the valley below carried forward by gravity.

Glaciers may appear static, but all are moving, even those in retreat. The middle section of the glacier generally moves the fastest; the bottom and sides are slowed by friction. Most glaciers move at a rate of about 3 feet per day; a retreating glacier is simply melting at a faster rate than it is moving forward. Occasionally, a glacier will "surge." In 1937, the Black Rapids Glacier in Alaska began flowing up to 216 feet per day; then, just as suddenly, it slowed to more typical glacial speeds and began to retreat.

Glaciers are vast conveyor belts of material plucked from the bedrock. Rocky debris is piled along lateral and medial moraines that streak the surface of the ice. Some rocks transported by glaciers can weigh thousands of tons and measure more than six-tenths of a mile in length; when dumped far from their point of origin, they are known as "erratics." Crevasses and fissures texture the glacier, and during the summer, meltwater on the surface collects in stunning blue ponds. This intense blue is mirrored in the densest portions of the glacier where the ice absorbs all but the blue part of the light spectrum, reflecting azure that even a tropical sky cannot match.

Glaciers and ice sheets move material. In one sense they destroy the land, in another sense they create it. Ice has left its mark in the form of striations and grooves on granite and in vast U-shaped valleys. Hanging valleys that once held a tributary glacier now flow with white waterfalls that rush over cliffs made sheer by the action of ice. Coastal fjords allow the sea to penetrate where a glacier once stood, indenting the land with picturesque fingers of water. Elsewhere, retreating glaciers have left kettlehole lakes, eskers, and drumlins as the visible marks of ice long melted.

Mark Twain once said, "A man who keeps company with glaciers comes to feel tolerably insignificant by and by." Anyone who has hiked to the base of a moraine or stared at the mountain spires of the Alps or the Rockies cannot help agreeing.

Ice has shaped the land even where it is invisible. In Alaska, 80 percent of the land is underlain by permanently frozen ground—permafrost—as is 50 percent of Canada. In the Arctic, permafrost is revealed through geometrically patterned ground known as polygons and ice-cored pingos that rise from the middle of drained lake basins. Here, ice dictates the way that life exists. Frozen ground just 3 feet below the surface restricts the roots of plants and the activities of burrowing animals. Drainage is impeded by permafrost, and level, flat land rapidly becomes wetland come spring and the brief flush of summer.

As soon as ice or snow melts, it begins its journey back to the sea. It may detour along the way, meandering through languid bends that loop slowly across the land. It may hesitate amid the deeper waters of a lake or seep through the confines of a riverbank to water grass or trees. Or it may rush forth in white, frantic motion, hardly delaying in its journey from mountain snow melt to reunion with its salty progenitor.

Rivers come in all shapes and sizes. They are straight, meandering, or braided. The flow of water cuts into the ground, carving a V-shaped valley that both confines the river to its banks and provides it with sustenance in the form of runoff from the surrounding drainage basin. Beyond the river, a larger floodplain may suggest that a greater power is at work in the regular flooding that erodes far beyond the riverbank. Large-scale flooding deposits sediments carried by the river; farming cultures around the world have long taken advantage of such regular gifts from the water. Along the Amazon, flooding may inundate the surrounding forest for 31 miles on either side of the river, blurring the distinction between river and land. Here, countless plants rely on the regular infusion of nutrients born by the floodwaters, and fish that feed on the forest floor have evolved.

Rivers are not simply channels for water to flow from their source to the ocean—they are integral parts of the ecosystem. They may disappear below ground, carving out underground worlds of caves and tunnels, dissolving rock to create mysterious labyrinths. In arid areas, the river may succumb to evaporation or filter down to join subterranean aquifers. In other regions, rivers may spring to life once again as the water table intersects with the surface and water wells upward.

Waterfalls are probably the most stunning riverine features. They are the visual embodiment of what happens when water and gravity collide. Gravity always wins such an encounter, as an explosion of water sends lacy fingers of liquid across rock and thundering clouds of mist skyward. The highest waterfall in the world is Angel Falls in southeastern Venezuela with a vertical drop of 2,625 feet. Other waterfalls may lack its height, but they still harbor beauty in their names: Bridalveil Falls, Silver Strand, Fairy, Feather. When David Livingston discovered a great falls along the Zambezi River in south central Africa, he named the 5,499-foot-wide, 361-foot-high falls after his monarch, Victoria. The African name is more emotive: *Mosioa-tunya* means "the smoke that thunders."

Waterfalls are relatively temporary displays of a river's strength. The cascading water forms a plunge pool beneath the falls, undercutting the rock and gradually moving the waterfall upstream, leaving a gorge in its wake. Niagara Falls is currently retreating at a rate of less than 3 feet a year; it will reach Lake Erie, 20 miles away, in about 50,000 years.

We have many names for the water that flows within a channel: river, stream, brook, creek, rivulet, bourne, rill, burn, beck, runnel. They are poetic distinctions more than hydrological ones. "I chatter, chatter as I flow," wrote Alfred, Lord Tennyson, "To join the brimming river, / For men may come, and men my go, / But I go on forever."

About 2,500 years ago, Heraclitus wrote: "You cannot step twice in the same river, for fresh waters are ever flowing upon you." Worldwide, rivers transport 153 cubic feet of water each year (that's 28 trillion gallons every day); even so, rivers only contain 0.025 percent of Earth's fresh-water liquid at any one time. Water is not the only thing rivers move. Through the power of erosion—the solvent action of water and abrasion—river waters move the land. The Mississippi River, 3,732 miles in length, transports an annual load between 350 million and 500 million tons. The Huang Ho, China's Yellow River, moves more than 1.6 billion tons a year, while the Ganges-Brahmaputra transports almost 3 billion tons. And what rivers erode, they must also deposit, fertilizing floodplains, creating vast deltas, swamps, and wetlands, and filling lakes.

Like waterfalls, lakes are but temporary features of the landscape. Many come into existence only after heavy rains; when the rains stop, they simply evaporate or drain away. Even those lakes that seem permanent will eventually vanish or be transformed, many filled in by sediments deposited by their source river, others succumbing to a change in climate or drainage patterns.

Lakes such as the Caspian Sea and Siberia's Lake Baikal exist in basins formed by movements in Earth's crust. Others are found in the craters of extinct volcanoes, such as Oregon's stunning Crater Lake, or dammed behind lava flows, as in the case of Yellowstone Lake. Lakes of glacial origin are found from the English Lake District to the Great Lakes of North America. Oxbow lakes are the cast-off meanders of wandering rivers.

Lakes share many features with the rivers that service them and the oceans that dwarf them. Most lakes receive their water from a river and lose it to a river. If no such input or output is present, the lake may lose its water by evaporation and gain it from groundwater. Some lakes are veritable seas in their own right. Just forty of the world's lakes contain four-fifths of all the freshwater held in lake basins, including Lake Baikal, Lake Tanganyika in Africa's Great Rift Valley, the Great Lakes, and Lake Victoria in east central Africa.

Lakes provide drinking water and have been tapped for power. They are host to commercial fisheries and recreational enthusiasts. And some lakes are simply beautiful to behold.

"A lake is the landscape's most beautiful and expressive feature," said Henry David Thoreau, writing of Walden Pond. "It is the earth's eye; looking into which the beholder measures the depth of his own nature." Water, it seems, can have a profound effect on the way we look at the world, if we allow our eyes to see.

After resting momentarily in the cradling basin of a lake, water continues on its way, flowing inevitably toward the sea. Wetlands and deserts may punctuate its course, the former filled with creatures and plants well adapted to a profusion of water, the latter to its virtual absence.

Mangroves send out aerial roots that grow up instead of down, so they don't get waterlogged. Marshes are filled with aquatic plants that can survive complete submersion, while in boglands, plants deal with a lack of essential elements by becoming carnivorous. In the desert, beetles drink the water that condenses on their own bodies at dawn; kangaroo rats thrive despite a complete lack of drinking water, relying instead on metabolic water and spending their time in burrows where humidity is high. In the hot Namib Desert, fairy shrimp live their brief lives in pools flooded by rare rains, laying eggs that can lay dormant for a single year or a century. No matter how much water is present, life invariably finds a way to survive and prosper.

As rivers finally reach the sea, they form deltas and estuaries, edge habitats that represent the union of waters. Biological productivity explodes in these regions. Ninety percent of the world's marine fish catch depends on coastal habitats for at least a part of its life cycle; mangroves, swamps, deltas, estuaries, and coral reefs all are essential to a healthy marine ecosystem.

Today, 2.7 billion people live within 62 miles of the coast. Most of the world's cities sit along waterways or within sight of the ocean. Ancient civilizations arose on the banks of rivers: the Sumerians between the Tigris and Euphrates in Iraq, the Harrapans along the Indus in Pakistan, the Chinese along the Hwang Ho and the Yangtze, and the Egyptians on the Nile. Modern civilization remains just as dependent on, and sometimes just as vulnerable to, the forces of tides and currents.

Our waters are under threat. Pollution by oil, pesticides, raw sewage, heavy metals, plastics, radioactive waste, and other chemicals is increasing as the human population increases. Acute pollution kills quickly and visibly, but more insidious chronic pollution can take longer to detect. One fifth of the world's population depends on fish as its sole source of protein, but many of the globe's fisheries are already overexploited. Mass wastage from unwanted by-catch and vessels that "efficiently" strip-mine the waters are depleting nontarget species at alarming rates. Less than 1 percent of marine areas are protected worldwide, and the coastal systems that are so vital to ocean fisheries are among the most seriously threatened of all habitats as they compete with human development for space.

Rivers and lakes bear the brunt of many of our demands for water: agricultural, industrial, domestic, and municipal. Rivers have been diverted, their channels blocked to create artificial reservoirs, or dredged to facilitate vessel passage. Unique systems such as Lake Baikal are under assault from industrial pollution, while others like California's Mono Lake are threatened by drainage to provide municipal water. Other waterways have been forever altered by the accidental or deliberate introduction of alien species that have out-competed native fish or clogged streams and ponds with destructive weeds. Lakes have been "overfertilized" by runoff from farmland, acidified by industrial by-products, and heated by power plants that use their water as a coolant.

As forests have been cleared from the land and replaced by farmland and pasture, the nature of water runoff has changed. With less vegetation to capture rainfall and snowmelt, more reaches rivers and streams. Overgrazing destroys vegetation, and with a loss of vegetation, the land gradually gets drier and drier. At its most extreme, the land turns to desert. People may try to put off the inevitable through irrigation and tapping into underground aquifers fed by ancient rains. But as much as we try to deny it, a desert is a desert.

However, there is an even larger problem now facing humanity. It is still a widely debated issue, but most scientists agree that emissions of so-called greenhouse gases are having an effect on Earth's climate, although no one knows how bad it may get. As carbon dioxide, water vapor, and certain other gases are released into the atmosphere, they trap the heat radiated from Earth, warming it. Without this naturally occurring global warming phenomenon, Earth would be far colder and much less hospitable than it is today. The concern is that human activities, particularly the burning of fossil fuels, are adding to natural greenhouse gas levels, resulting in an increase in global temperature.

Temperatures have risen and fallen for millennia, as have sea levels. The problem is that such changes could now occur over a much shorter timeframe. The Intergovernmental Panel on Climate Change, a committee of more than 2,500 scientists from around the world, has estimated future warming levels of between 34° Fahrenheit and 38° Fahrenheit over the next century. The sea level rise that could accompany that increase has been estimated at anywhere from 8 inches to a foot. Humans have survived far greater fluctuations in the past, but we now have a world population approaching 6 billion, with a projection of close to 11 billion by the twenty-third century, the majority of whom will be living near the coast in some of the most vulnerable areas.

We may have an ally in this climacteric conundrum: water. The oceans moderate extreme temperature changes, acting as vast reservoirs of heat. They also serve as a sink for carbon dioxide, taking fully one-half of the carbon dioxide produced by combustion out of atmospheric circulation and reducing the likelihood of large-scale climate change. However, some researchers believe that the oceans may at times relinquish their carbon dioxide load, releasing it into the atmosphere with catastrophic effects; the Permian mass extinction 245 million years ago, which eliminated 90 percent of ocean genera, half of all marine families, and 75 percent of all amphibian and reptile families, has been attributed by some to just such a release.

As the next millennium dawns, a new generation of explorers are charting the oceans, while thousands of miles above us the Mir space station and NASA's Space Shuttle continue to give us views of our planet that cannot help making us humble. Skyward, we are learning of the ice cores of comets that may once have fed ancient seas with extraterrestrial water and of the frozen oceans of Mars where life may once have flourished long before our own seas. Back on Earth we are learning that we have more questions than answers, and that curiosity may be our most important character trait.

From the depths of the oceans to the middle of the desert, from the glacial mountain peaks to V-shaped river valleys, and from the coral reef atolls of the South Pacific to the Antarctic ice shelf, water in all of its forms dominates Earth. Thomas Fuller, a seventeenth-century writer said, "We never know the worth of water till the well is dry." With the many threats and challenges facing the world's water supply, those words have proved prophetic.

As our population continues to grow, our coasts, rivers, lakes, aquifers, and oceans are facing almost insurmountable pressures. They receive what we discard, and still we expect them to flow with crystal clarity, provide us with food, irrigate our crops, and cleanse our land with rain.

What does water mean to the human psyche? It is liquid imagination. Water inspired Thales of Miletus, the first Greek philosopher. It has inspired great writers: Shakespeare, Coleridge, Thoreau, Emerson, Conrad, Melville, and Steinbeck. It has even inspired modern-day writers and filmmakers, from Peter Benchley to Steven Spielberg.

The sight of a thundering white waterfall, an immense blue iceberg, or the simple setting of the Sun turning the ocean golden is enough to light the spark of imagination and an appreciation of beauty in our minds. Sometimes, though, we are tempted to look only at the water's surface. We can forget that much lies below, out of sight, or dissolved in imperfect solution. We have the chance to see our successes and our failures in how we treat water. There is success in a river filled with returning salmon, and there is failure in an ever-sinking water table and encroaching desert.

As we move forward into another era of exploration, in which the names of our spacecraft—*Columbia, Challenger, Discovery, Atlantis,* and *Endeavour*—mirror the names of early vessels of exploration, there are two things that we will never be able to exist without—the heat from some distant star and water. Water is the most abundant substance on the surface of Earth; it is also the most precious. Simply put—all the wealth of the world pales beside an oasis in the desert. Between Heaven and Earth, there is water.

We never know the worth of water till the well is dry.

THOMAS FULLER, GNOMOLOGIA, *5451*

DEW ON GRASS, *Unalaska Island, Alaska*

MOUNTAIN STREAM AND PINK MONKEY FLOWERS (*MIMULOUS LEWISII*), Mt. Rainier National Park, Washington

BIGLEAF MAPLE *(ACER MACROPHYLLUM)* LEAF IN CURRENT, *Snoqualmie River, Washington*

AUTUMN LANDSCAPE WITH MAPLES *(ACER SPP.)*, *Honshu, Japan*

So was it with these stones; the ocean is their eternity,

and each note of that wild music told of one more step

towards their destiny.

CHARLES DARWIN, VOYAGE OF THE 'BEAGLE'

RAPIDS, SOL DUC RIVER, *Olympic National Park, Washington*

MOUNTAIN STREAM,
Grandfather Mountain,
North Carolina

MOUNTAIN STREAM,
*Mt. Assiniboine Provincial
Park, Alberta, Canada*

31

WATERFALL, *Switzerland*

WATERFALL, *Bwindi Rainforest, Uganda*

My eyes had never before beheld such beauty in a mountain stream. The water was almost as transparent as the air—was, indeed, like liquid air; and it lay in these wells and pits enveloped in shadow, or lit up by a chance ray of vertical sun, it was a perpetual feast to the eye—so cool, so deep, so pure; every reach and pool like a vast spring.

JOHN BURROUGHS

WATERFALL, *Unalaska Island, Alaska*

RAPIDS,
Yosemite National Park,
California

WATERFALL,
Icy Bay, Alaska

WATERFALL, *Yosemite National Park, California*

WATERFALL, *Unalaska Island, Alaska*

He shall come down like rain upon the mown

grass: as showers that water the earth.

Psalms 72:6

WATERFALL, *Niobrara River Valley, Nebraska*

RAPIDS, *Sol Duc River, Olympic National Park, Washington*

GIANT STEPS WATERFALL, *Paradise Valley, Banff National Park, Alberta, Canada*

The mystery of language was revealed to me. I knew then that 'w-a-t-e-r' meant the wonderful cool something that was flowing over my hand. That living word awakened my soul, gave it light, joy, set it free!

HELEN KELLER, *THE STORY OF MY LIFE*

RAPIDS REFLECTING AUTUMN COLORS,
Queets River, Olympic National Park, Washington

YANOMAMO HUNTER, *Tapirapeco National Park, Venezuela*

RAPIDS REFLECTING AUTUMN COLORS, *Queets River, Olympic National Park, Washington*

BROWN BEARS *(URSUS ARCTOS)*, *Katmai National Park, Alaska*

RAPIDS,
Escalante River, Utah

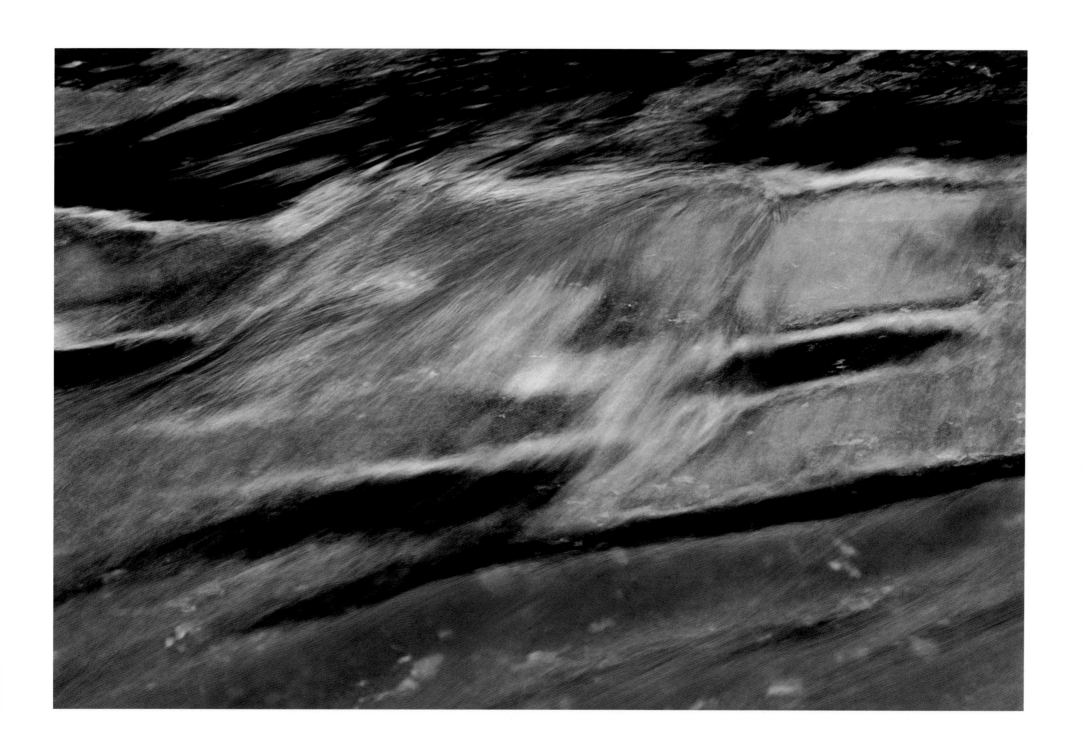

REFLECTIONS, *Escalante River, Utah*

RAPIDS, *Escalante River, Utah* 55

RAPIDS, *Sol Duc River, Olympic National Park, Washington*

SURF AT SUNSET, *Pacific Coast, Oregon*

COTTONGRASS *(ERIOPHORUM SPP.)* IN ALPINE POND, *Rocky Mountains, Alberta, Canada*

SNOWY EGRET *(EGRETTA THULA)*, *Ding Darling National Wildlife Refuge, Florida*

BURCHELL'S ZEBRA *(EQUUS BURCHELLI)* AT WATERHOLE, *Etosha National Park, Namibia*

CLOUD REFLECTIONS, *Everglades National Park, Florida*

Great, wide beautiful, wonderful world,

With the wonderful water round you curled…

WILLIAM BRIGHTY RANDS, "THE CHILD'S WORLD"

YANOMAMO BOY, *Tapirapeco National Park, Venezuela*

SAN BUSHMAN COLLECTING WATER, *Kalahari Desert, Botswana*

DANI WOMEN COLLECTING SALT, *Highlands, Balem Valley, Irian Jaya*

GRAIN MILL AND WATER WHEEL, *Glendale, Isle of Skye, Scotland*

RICE TERRACES, *Bali*

NORTHERN RED OAK *(QUERCUS RUBRA)*, AMERICAN BEECH *(FAGUS GRANDIFOLIA)*, AND RED MAPLE *(ACER RUBRUM)* LEAVES, *North Carolina*

AUTUMN REFLECTIONS, *Sol Duc River, Olympic National Park, Washington*

In the golden lightning

Of the sunken Sun —

O'er which clouds are brightning,

Thou dost float and run;

Like an unbodied joy whose race is just begun.

PERCY BYSSHE SHELLEY, "TO A SKY-LARK"

SPECTACLED CAIMAN *(CAIMAN SCLEROPS)*, Napo-River-Region, Peru

AUTUMN REFLECTIONS, *Wynoochee River, Olympic National Park, Washington*

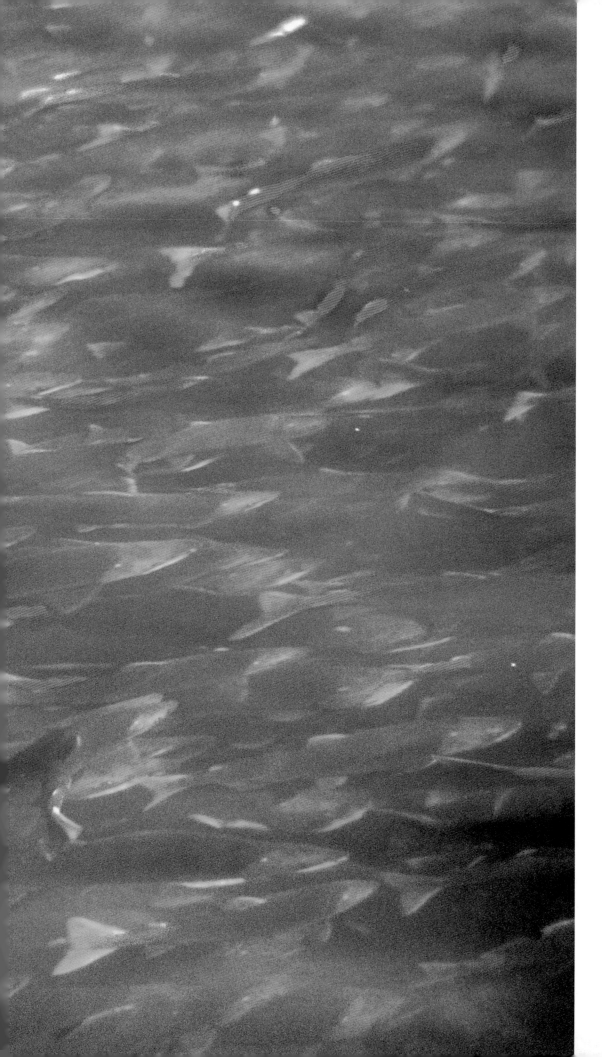

Ask why the sunlight not forever

Weaves rainbows o'er yon mountain river…

Percy Bysshe Shelley, "Hymn To Intellectual Beauty"

Sockeye salmon (*Oncorhyncus nerka*),
Hansen Creek, Wood River Lakes Region, Alaska

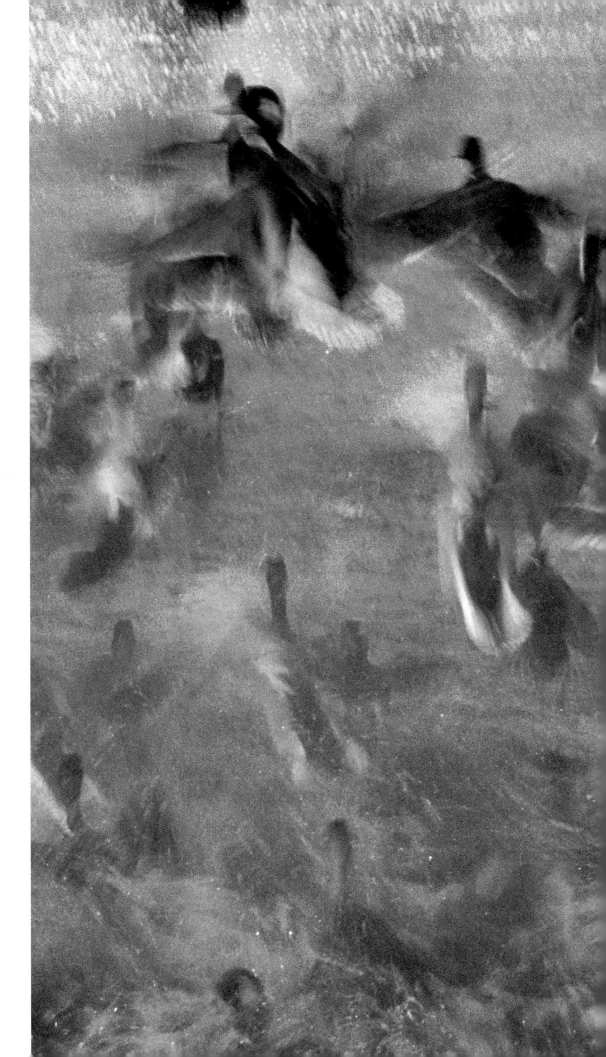

MALLARD DUCKS *(ANAS PLATYRHYNCHOS),*
Rifle Wildlife Refuge, British Columbia, Canada

HAMARA TRIBESMAN HERDING GOATS AND CATTLE, *Turmi, Ethiopia*

SUNRISE, *Lake Yellowstone, Yellowstone National Park, Wyoming*

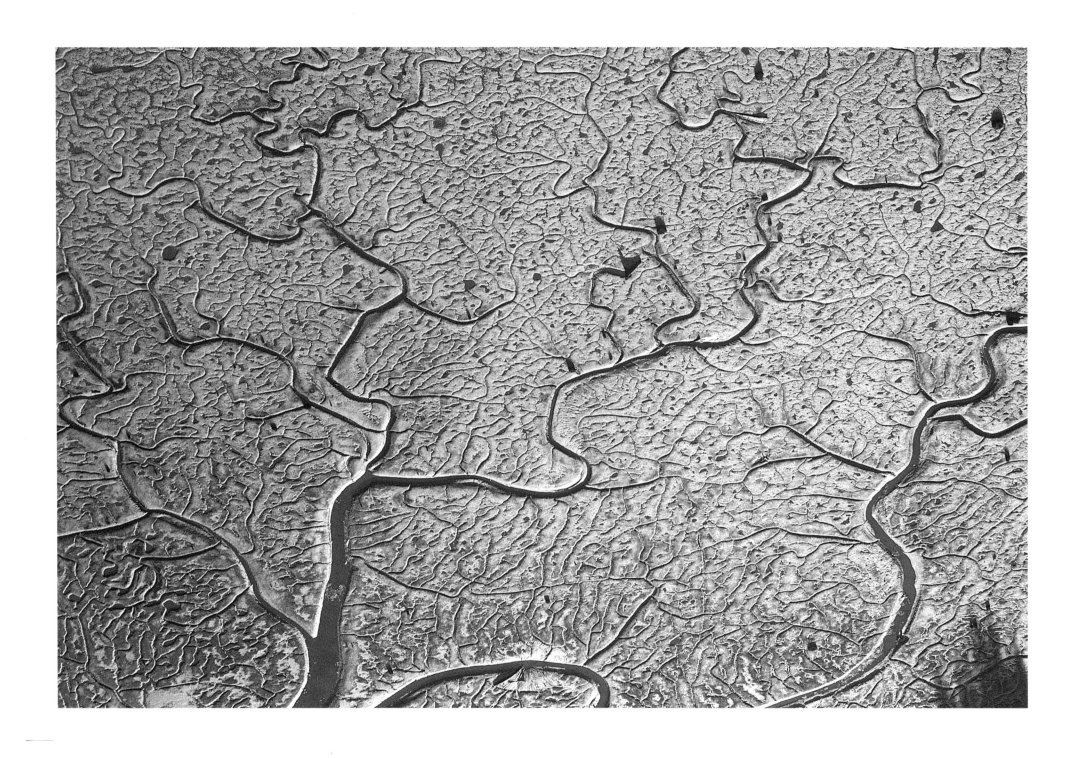

TIDAL FLATS, *Skagit River, Washington*

Nothing so fair, so pure, and at the same time so large, as a

lake, perchance, lies on the surface of the earth. Sky water.

It needs no fence.

Henry D. Thoreau, *Walden*

REFLECTIONS AND SILHOUETTES,
Marvel Lake, Mount Assiniboine Provincial Park, Alberta, Canada

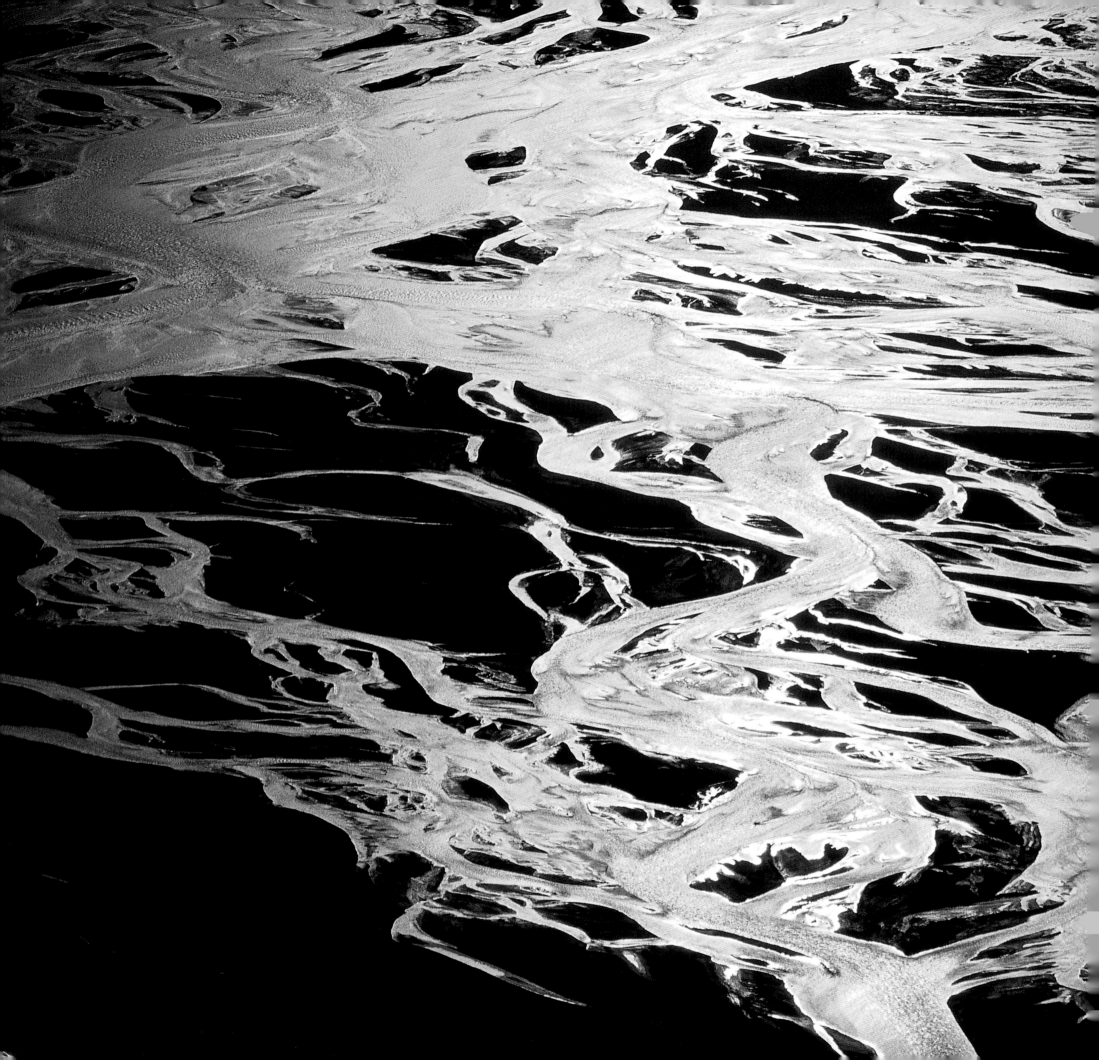

Water has some kind of powerful mystery about it. Still waters,

moving waters, dark waters; the words themselves have a

mysterious, almost dying fall.

H.E. Bates

TIDE LANDS, *Skagit River, Washington*

TUNDRA PONDS, *Arctic National Wildlife Refuge, Alaska*

On these shores there are echoes of past and future: of the flow

of time, obliterating yet containing all that has gone before; of

the sea's eternal rhythms — the tides, the beat of surf, the press-

ing rivers of the currents — shaping, changing, dominating; of

the stream of life, flowing as inexorably as any ocean current,

from past to unknown future.

RACHEL CARSON, THE EDGE OF THE SEA

OCEAN BEACH, *Olympic National Park, Washington*

The gentleness of heaven broods o'er the Sea…

WILLIAM WORDSWORTH, "IT IS A BEAUTEOUS EVENING"

RECEDING SURF, *Arctic National Wildlife Refuge, Alaska*

WAVE-WASHED ROCKS, *Olympic Peninsula, Washington*

CALIFORNIA SEA LIONS (*ZALOPHUS CALIFORNIANUS*), *California*

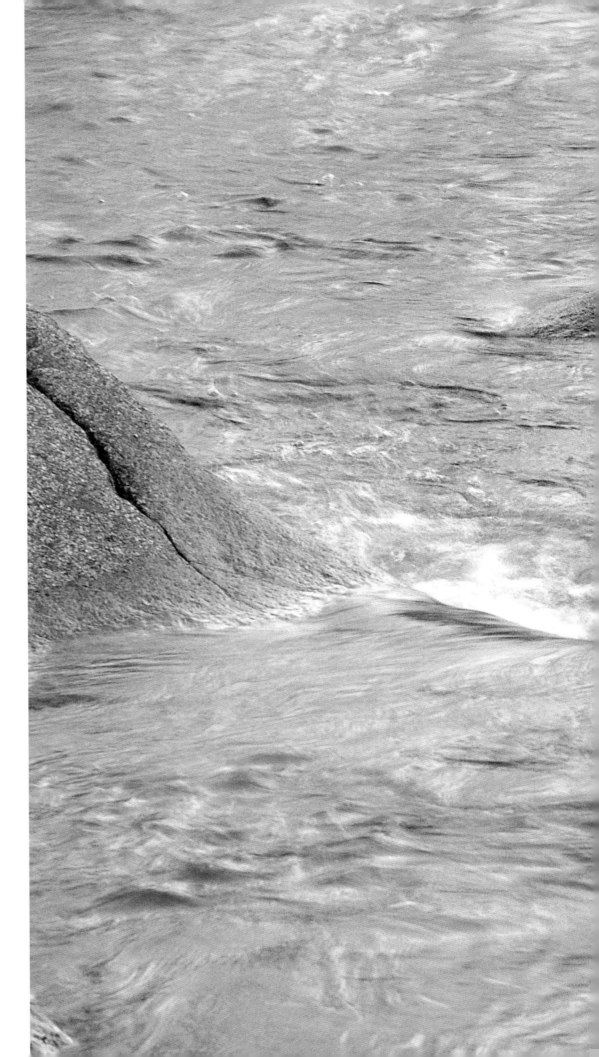

AUTUMN REFLECTIONS,
Sol Duc River, Olympic National Park, Washington

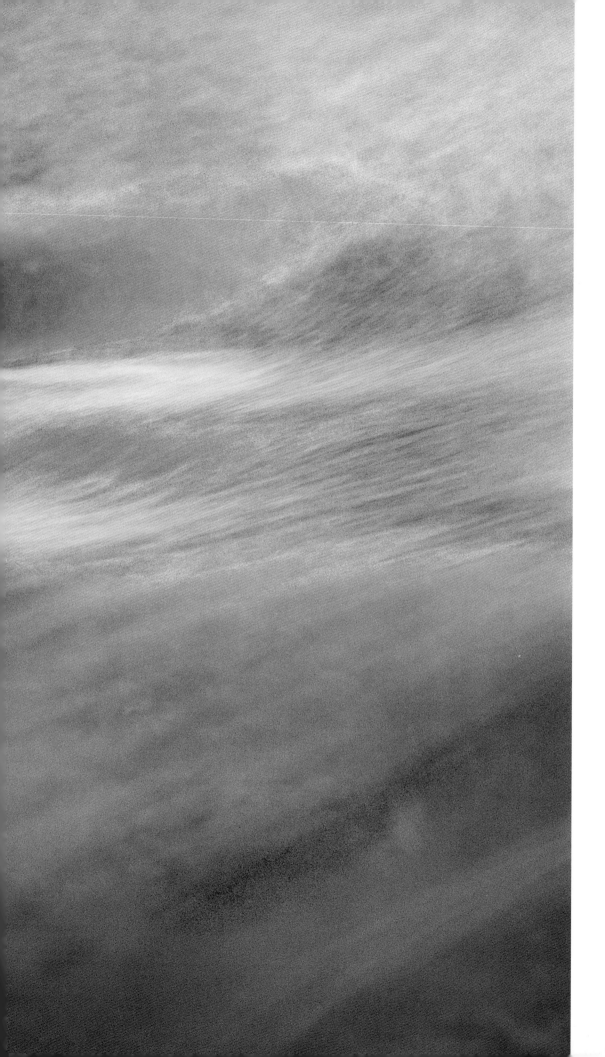

The conscious water saw its God and blushed.

RICHARD CRASHAW

PACIFIC WAVES, *Maui, Hawaii*

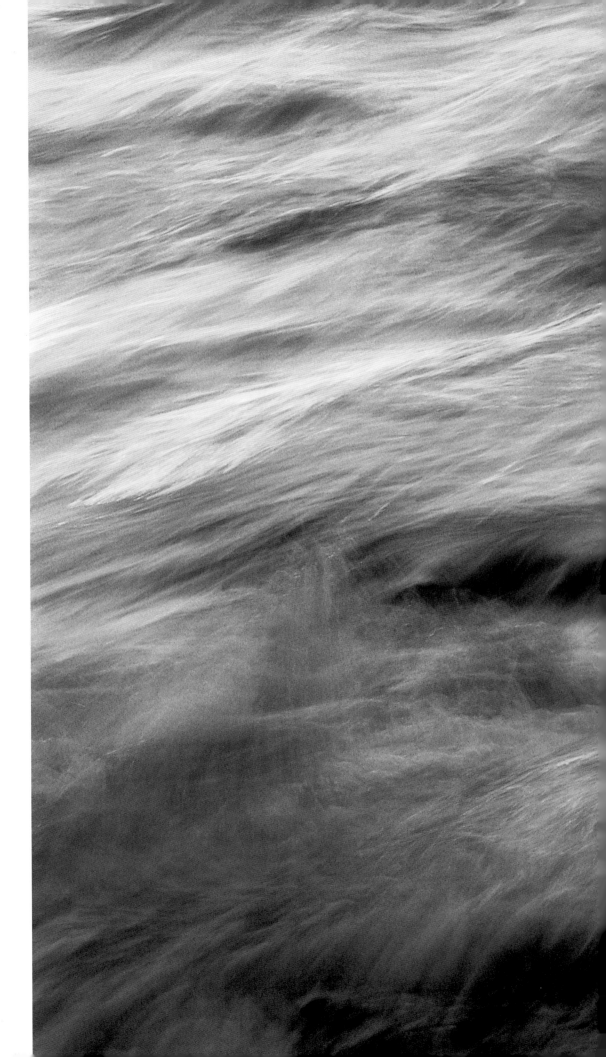

SURF, *Ruby Beach, Olympic National Park, Washington*

WALRUS (*ODOBENUS ROSMARUS*), Cape Pierce, Alaska

For the sea lies all about us....In its mysterious past it encompasses all the dim origins of life and receives in the end, after, it may be, many transmutations, the dead husks of that same life. For all at last return to the sea—to Oceanus, the ocean river, like the ever-flowing stream of time, the beginning, and the end.

Rachel Carson, *The Sea Around Us*

WAVES AT SUNSET, *Cannon Beach, Oregon*

WAVE, *Pacific Coast, Oregon*

SURF, *Pacific Coast, Oregon*

Roll on, thou deep and dark-blue ocean, roll!

Ten thousand fleets sweep over thee in vain;

Man marks the earth with ruin, his control

Stops with the shore;...

BYRON, "CHILDE HAROLD, IV"

SURF, *Pacific Coast, Oregon*

BELUGA WHALE
(*DELPHINAPTERUS LEUCAS*),
Arctic, Canada

WAVE, *Maui, Hawaii*

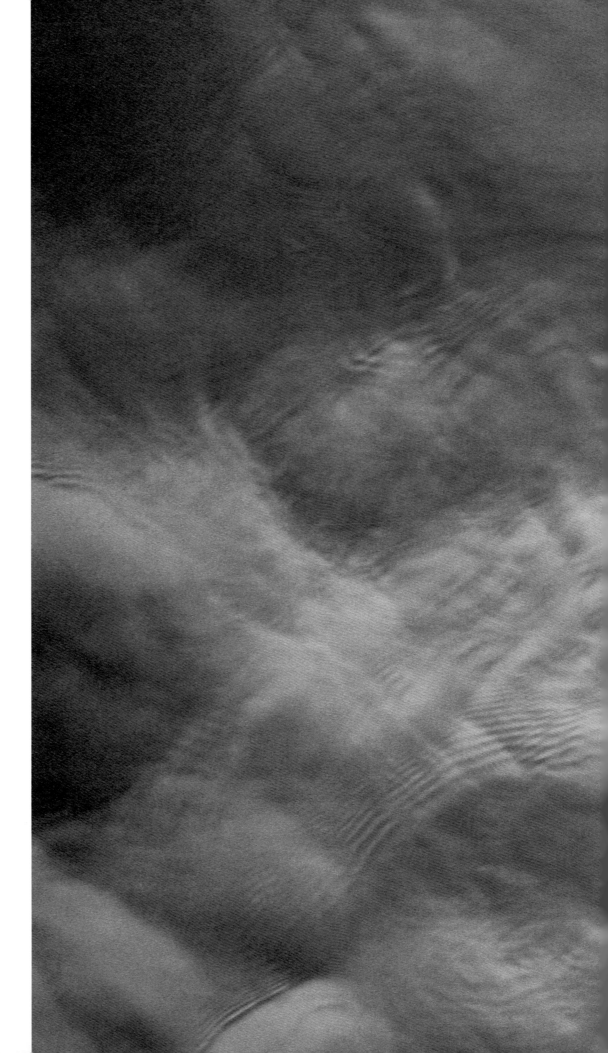

Nature never did betray the heart that loved her.

WILLIAM WORDSWORTH, "TINTERN ABBEY"

KING PENGUIN (*APTENODYTES PATAGONICUS*),
Macquarie Island, Antarctic

BELUGA WHALES (*DELPHINAPTERUS LEUCAS*), *Somerset Island, Canada*

WAVES, *Pacific Coast, Oregon*

WAVE, *Maui, Hawaii*

AERIAL VIEW OF ATOLL AND REEFS, *Bora Bora, French Polynesia*

TAHITIAN CHILDREN
IN A LAGOON,
Bora Bora, French Polynesia

HARBOR SEAL
(*PHOCA VITULINA*),
Pacific Northwest

Yonder, by the ever-brimming goblet's rim, the warm waves blush like wine. The gold brow plumbs the

blue. The diver sun — slow dived from noon — goes down; my soul mounts up!

Herman Melville, Moby Dick

RECEDING TIDE AT
SUNSET, SECOND BEACH,
Olympic National Park,
Washington

SEA STACKS, *Cannon Beach, Oregon*

ORCA (*ORCINUS ORCA*) HUNTING SOUTHERN SEA LIONS (*OTARIA FLAVESCENS*), *Peninsula Valdez, Argentina*

WAVES AND SEA STACK, *Second Beach, Olympic National Park, Washington*

SURF AND CLIFFS,
Big Sur, California

Common Dolphin *(Delphinus delphis)* Exhaling, *Sea of Cortez, Mexico*

AUTUMN REFLECTIONS,
Wynoochee River, Olympic National Park, Washington

HUMPBACK WHALE (*MEGAPTERA NOVAEANGLIAE*) DIVING, *Point Adolphus, Alaska*

FISHERMAN, *Indian Ocean, Mauritius*

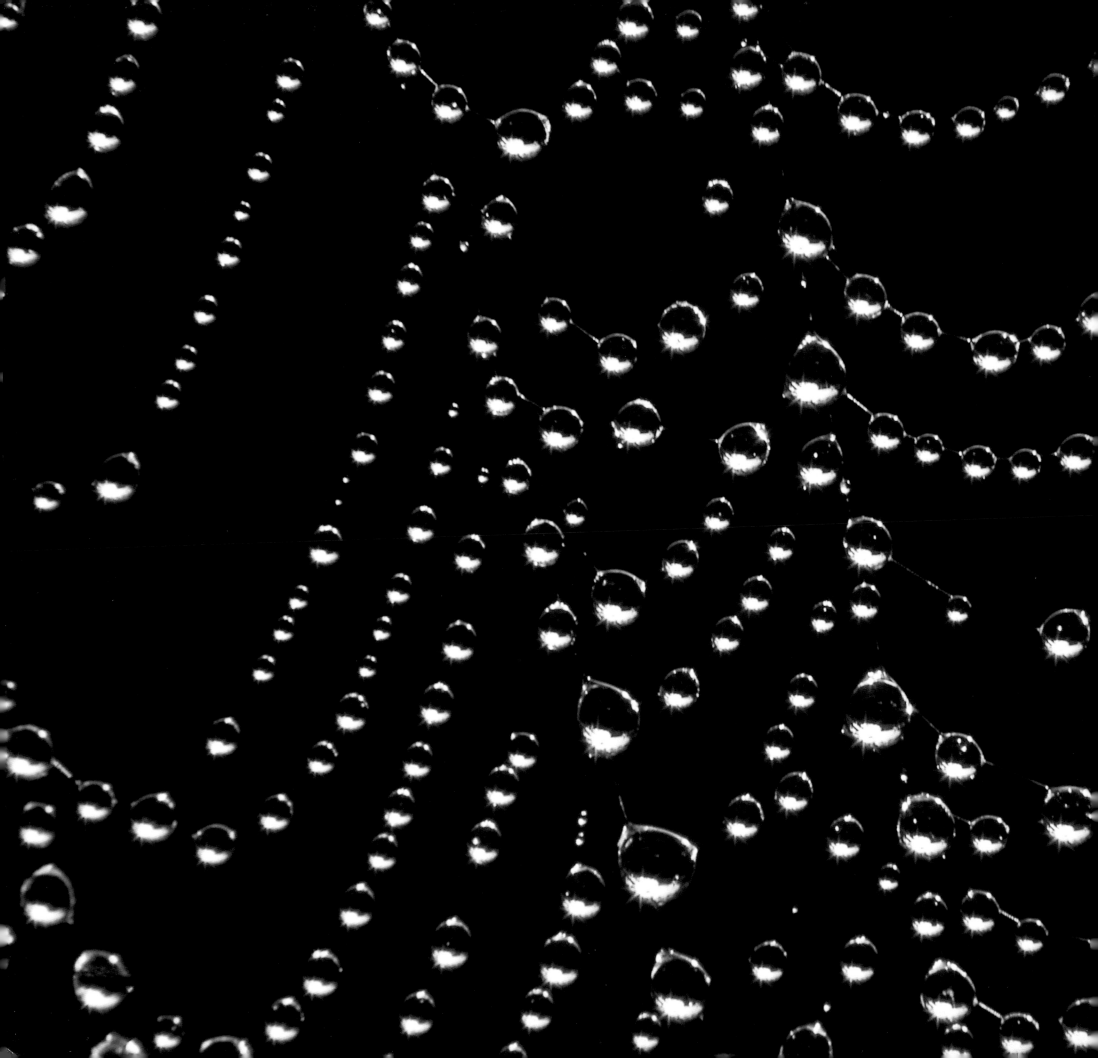

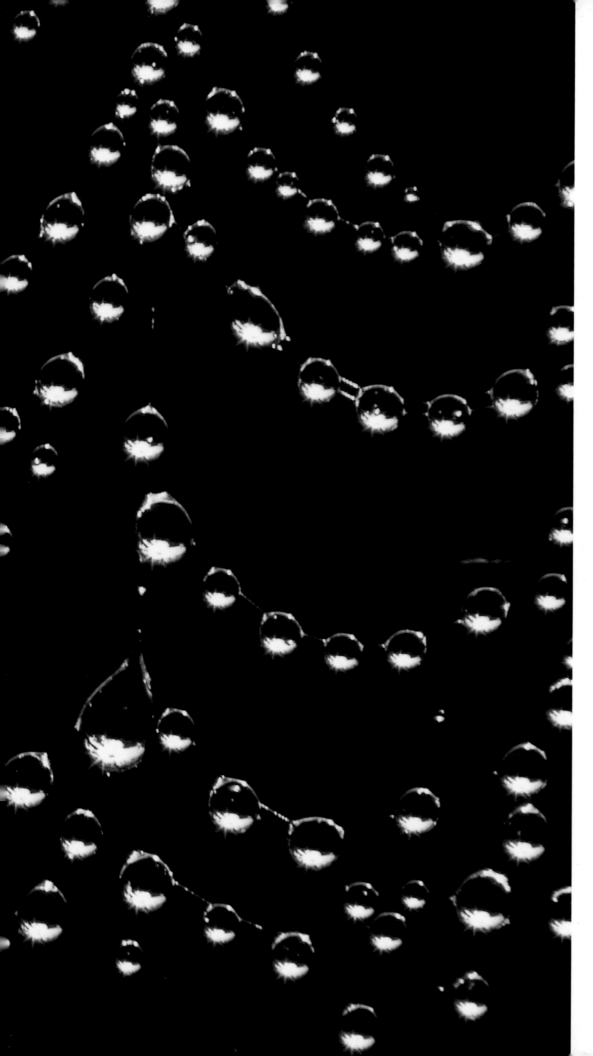

Little drops of water

Little grains of sand,

Make the mighty ocean

And the pleasant land.

Julia A. Fletcher Carney, "Little Things"

DEW DROPS ON THE WEB OF AN ORB WEB SPIDER
(*ARANEUS DIADEMATUS*), *Washington*

APPLE TREE *(MALUS SPP.)* IN THE FOG, *Romantic Road, Germany*

STORM AND CHURCH,
Wester Ross, Scotland

137

These is a pleasure in the pathless woods,

There is rapture on the lonely shore,

There is society when none intrudes,

By the deep sea, and music in its roar;

I love not Man the less, but Nature more…

Byron, "Childe Harold, IV"

DOUGLAS FIRS *(PSEUDOTSUGA MENZIESII)* IN THE FOG,
Olympic National Park, Washington

MOON WITH CLOUDS, *Tracy Arm, Alaska*

SPRING RAIN, *Washington*

PINES *(PINUS SPP.)* IN THE FOG,
Monte San Michele, Tuscany, Italy

RAIN FALLING IN TUNDRA POND, *Arctic National Wildlife Refuge, Alaska*

My heart leaps up when I behold

A rainbow in the sky.

WILLIAM WORDSWORTH, "MY HEART LEAPS UP"

RAINBOW, *New Mexico*

PINES *(PINUS SPP.)* AT SUNRISE, *Glacier National Park, Montana*

SUNRISE, *Amboseli National Park, Kenya*

I sift the snow on the mountains below,

And their great pines groan aghast;

And all the night 'tis my pillow white,

While I sleep in the arms of the blast.

PERCY BYSSHE SHELLEY, "THE CLOUD"

SNOWY LANDSCAPE, *Honshu, Japan*

BLACK COTTONWOOD *(POPULUS TRICHOCARPA)* LEAF IN ICE, *Canada*

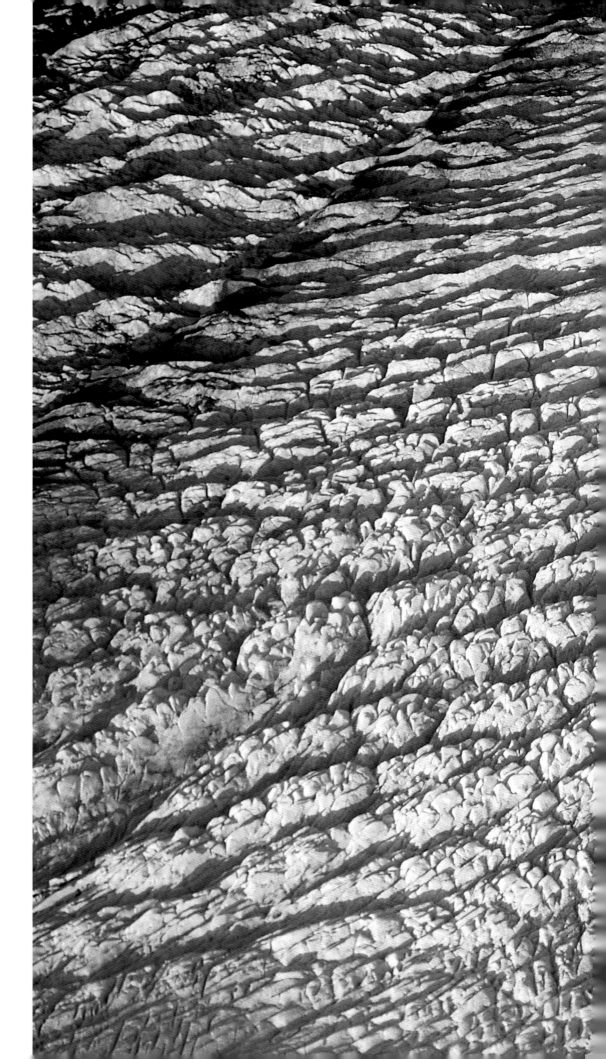

AERIAL VIEW OF MILES GLACIER, *Alaska*

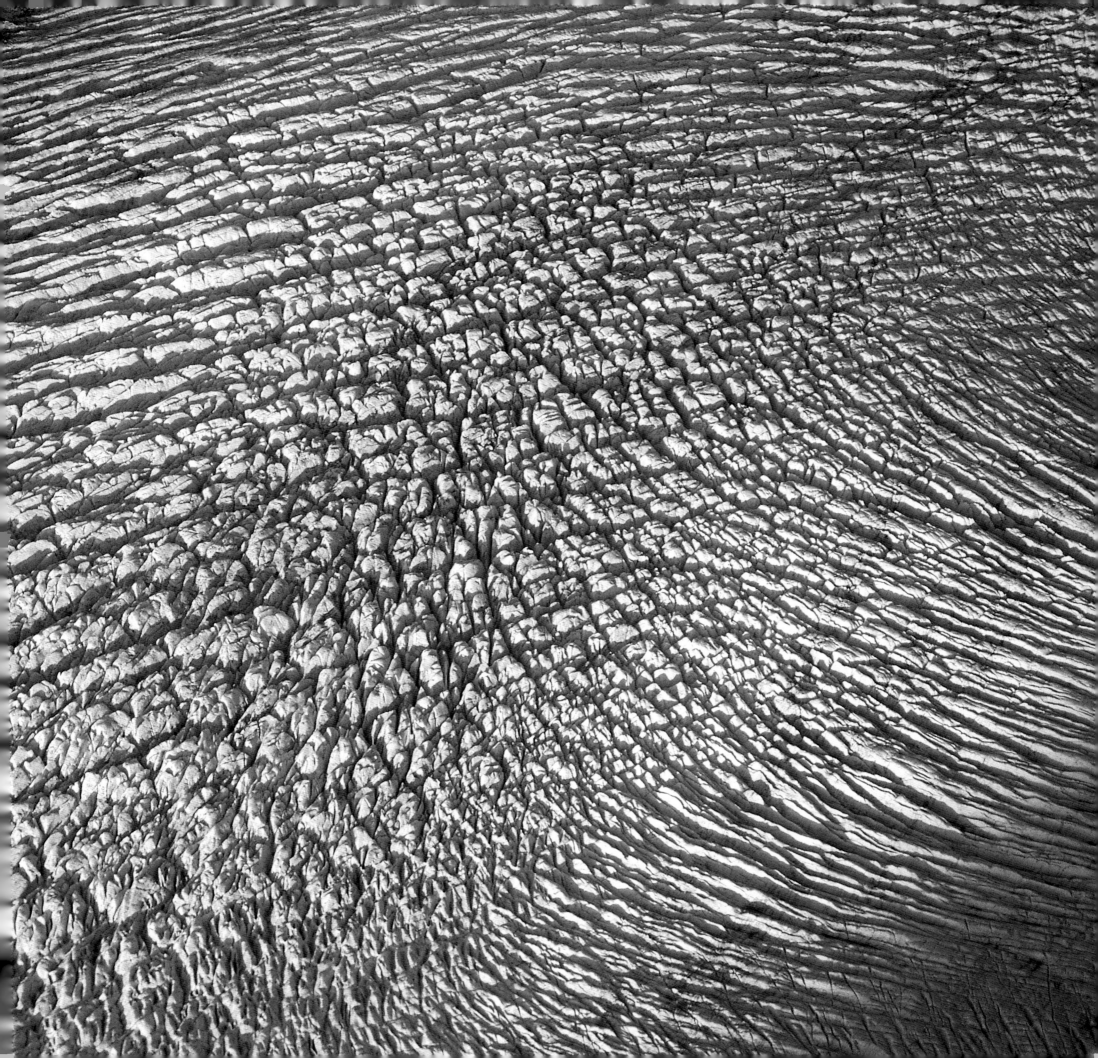

FROST ON PACIFIC
COAST SWORD FERN
(*POLYSTICHUM MUNITUM*) IN
THE RAINFOREST, *Olympic
National Park, Washington*

WINTER LANDSCAPE
WITH RED ALDERS (ALNUS
RUBRA), *Snoqualmie River,*
Washington

ICE AND STONES, *Washington*

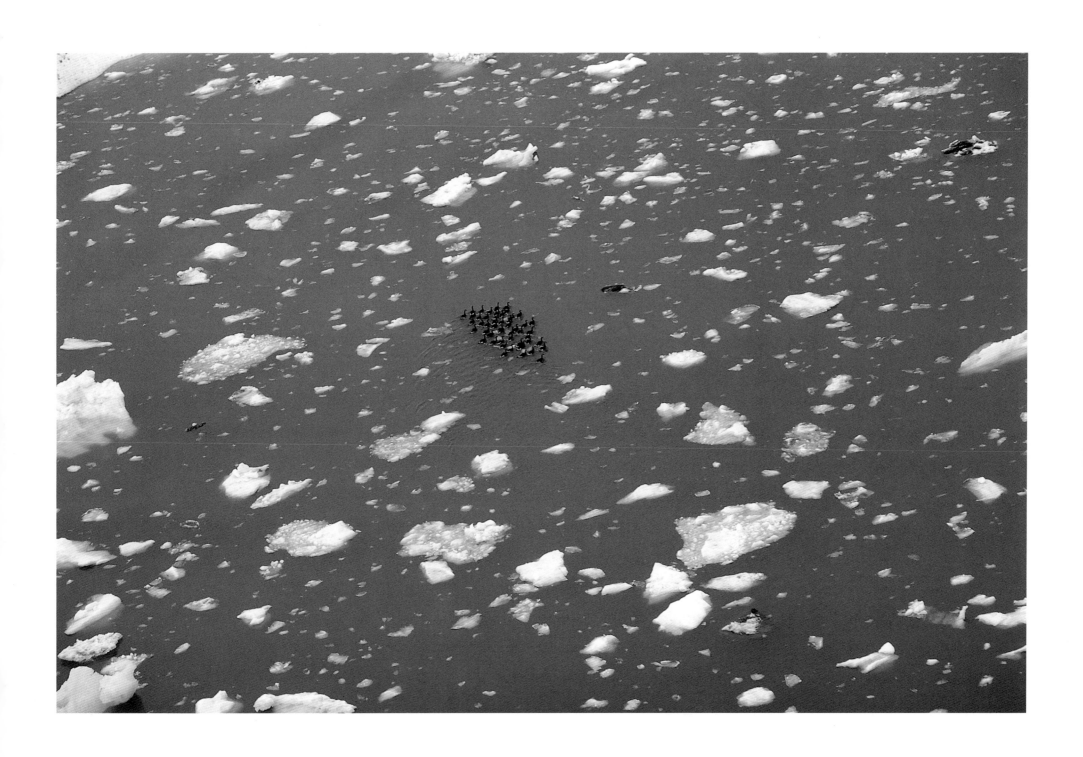

CANADA GEESE *(BRANTA CANADENSIS)* AND ICE FLOWS, *Alaska*

This iceberg cuts its facets from within.

Like jewelry from a grave

it saves itself perpetually and adorns

Only itself.

Elizabeth Bishop

Aerial view of Jefferies Glacier,
Wrangell-Saint Elias National Park and Preserve, Alaska

EAST RONGBUK GLACIER, *Himalayas, Tibet*

CARIBOU *(RANGIFER TARANDRUS)* IN BRAIDED RIVER, *Arctic National Wildlife Refuge, Alaska*

The ice was here, the ice was there,

The ice was all around:

It cracked and growled, and roared and howled,

Like noises in a sound!

SAMUEL TAYLOR COLERIDGE

ICEBERGS, *Copper River, Alaska*

Water is good; it benefits all things and does not compete with them.

Lao-tzu, *The Way of Lao-tzu*

HARBOR SEAL *(PHOCA VITULINA)* ON THE ICE, *Tracy Arm, Alaska*

Icebergs behoove the soul

(both being self-made from elements least visible)

to see them so: fleshed, fair, erected, indivisible.

ELIZABETH BISHOP

ICEBERG, *Tracy Arm, Alaska*

ADELIE PENGUINS *(PYGOSCELIS ADELIAE), Antarctica*

EAST RONGBUK GLACIER, *Himalayas, Tibet*

ICEBERGS, *Prince William Sound, Alaska*

ADELIE PENGUINS (*PYGOSCELIS ADELIAE*), *Antarctica*

The face of water, in time, became a wonderful book —

a book that was a dead language to the uneducated

passenger, but which told its mind to me without reserve,

delivering its most cherished secrets as clearly as if it utte-

red them with a voice. And it was not a book to

be read once and thrown aside, for it had a new story

to tell every day.

MARK TWAIN, *LIFE ON THE MISSISSIPPI*

AUF ICE, *Hulahula River, Arctic National Wildlife Refuge, Alaska*

AERIAL VIEW OF MILES GLACIER, *Alaska*

AERIAL VIEW OF GLACIER, *Fairweather Range, Alaska*

ICE CAVE,
Glacier Bay. Alaska

"All are but parts of one stupendous Whole;

Whose body Nature is, and God the soul.

Pope, Essay on Man, I

KING PENGUINS (*APTE-NODYTES PATAGONI-CUS*), *South Georgia Island, United Kingdom*

Let thy west wind sleep on

The Lake; speak silence with thy glimmering eyes,

And wash the dusk with silver.

WILLIAM BLAKE, "TO THE EVENING STAR"

ICEBERGS AND THE ALSEK GLACIER, *St. Elias Mountains, Alaska*   183

STRANDED ICEBERG,
Icy Bay, Alaska

GLACIAL LAKE,
Alaska

When Will Rivers Sue?

By Claus Biegert

Two men stand along the banks of the Cuyahoga River. They talk about America before and after the arrival of the European settlers. From differing points of view, they speak of their land. One of the two men is a Native American.

The man of European heritage asks the Native American: "What would you have ever made out of this country if we hadn't came over from Europe? Most likely you would have left it the way it was. At least we turned this country really into something."

The Indian doesn't answer immediately. His eyes wander the river to stop at the signs lining its banks. The signs prohibit the throwing of cigarette butts or the disposal of glowing rubbish into the river. As it winds through Cleveland, the Cuyahoga River takes on so many inflammable chemicals that its surface is hazed with a film—a film that in the summer heat can go up in flames.

Finally, his gaze piqued by the scene, the Indian answers: "You're probably right. We never would have dreamed up the idea of having a burning river flow through our land."

The meeting took place toward the end of the 1960s. The Indian was Vine Deloria, Jr., a gifted attorney, historian, and theologian of the Lakota who was born on the Standing Rock Reservation. The episode of the inflammable river opens his appeal, "We Talk, You Listen."

Our civilization has transformed its drinking springs into ornamental fountains. Quite often a sign reminds us: *Water Not Potable*. Water that arrives so dependably through the tap allows us no insight into its quality of character. Water pipes laid by the water utility are in touch with the source—not us.

Bearing this broken connection in mind, the elders of the Hopi village of Hotevilla (located in the highlands of Arizona) fought a bitter battle against the implementation of a public water system. "Only when we can visit the source," say the Hopi, "can we accord water the respect it's due and use it honorably." According to the elders, children who only see the water that comes from the faucet—water that's been piped for miles into their homes—can have no real understanding of water's essence.

Indigenous people from around the globe tell us that water is sacred. The Maori of New Zealand waged a legal battle on behalf of their rivers. They won, defeating public plans to build a sewage treatment plant along the banks of the Kaituna—a river they hold holy. From the Maori point of view, it is unimaginable that effluents and treated wastes should be channeled into a natural body of water. One of the Kaituna's defenders is Eva Waitiki: "We told the judges about our river, its power, its uniqueness. We told them that the Kaituna is like a brother to us. We even spoke of the *Taniwha,* the protecting water spirits. We explained to them that the sicknesses of the soul, which we call *Mate Maori,* can only be healed by a healthy river. And that flushing treated water into the Kaituna would be to rob it of its healing nature and to take away the hopes of those who are sick."

Eva Waitiki was once brought to the Kaituna to be cured: "When I was seven years old, I stepped on a shard of glass and badly lacerated my foot. The White doctor said that I would be lame for life. Then the elders brought me to the Kaituna. I remember that they submerged me entirely, remember the clear water surging over me. They repeated this every day, and after two weeks my foot was completely healed."

Water cleanses and heals. Ancient Egyptian mythology speaks of Ra, the Sun God, purifying himself in the ocean beyond the sky before setting off on his daily journey. According to the Germanic sagas, the earth springs of Weltenesche Yggdrasil turn every object dipped into them a white that amazes. Before the Last Supper, Jesus washed the feet of his disciples. The midwives of Old Mexico would wash newborn infants while praying that the water cleanse away all the evils inherited from the parents. The Aztec City of Tenochtitlàn (which stood at the site now occupied by Mexico City—a metropolis plagued by water shortages) possessed three sacred baths in which the Priest Kings of Tollan would bathe in a midnight ritual. Sinai Bedouins—although water is precious— wash themselves before entering into prayer. For people of the Hindu religion, the pilgrimage to the holy rivers is one of the most sacred duties. While underway, Japanese who visit the Shinto shrines on Ise wash their hands and rinse out their mouths in the waters of the Isuzu River. To purify their bodies and souls, the Indians of North America go into sweat lodges to chant and sing as vapor rises from the hot stones. Catholic Christians sprinkle themselves with holy water upon entering church. But for the most part in the Western World—discounting the various water spa treatments or the teachings of Sebastian Kneipp—the understanding of water's symbolic cleansing and healing power is almost forgotten. When Joseph Beuys on Easter of 1985 in Switzerland, citing the importance of the Sermon of the Mount, washed his feet in a ritual act, the scene was met with incomprehension.

What is so sacred about water? Why do the peoples of nonindustrial societies attach such significance to water? The time has arrived to extend our investigations beyond water's well-known chemical and physical layers.

The life-giving property of water is its unusual facility to dissolve other substances. Water doesn't destroy these substances, but instead fragments them, conserves them, carries them along. Water vitalizes nature's necessary life-giving organic components. Water floods cells and organisms, washes the entire biosphere with nutrients, sweeps away toxic substances. Water regulates the metabolism of the organism and protects it from overheating as carbohydrates are burned. Water constitutes 60 percent of the human body. Particularly important organs such as the brain, made up of 75 percent water, are thought of as being relatively saturate; the bones, made up of 23 percent water, are considered dry.

It is the flow of water that fuels its mystique. The motion of water, its rhythmic movement, helps unleash its hydrometabolism. Whether we watch a brook, a river, the ocean waves—or whether we merely regard the whirlpool gurgling above the bathtub's shiny drain—we witness water's fascinating undulations. Through its pulsing oscillations, water both accumulates and unleashes energy. The molecules bond newly, change configurations, unite or—the electrical polarities always seeking new partners, positive seeking negative, negative seeking positive—pull free. These ionic variations inscribe the liquid's electromagnetic structure. This structure changes according to temperature: seethed to a boil, it turns into steam; chilled to a standstill, it turns into ice.

Water's electromagnetic signature is conditioned by local events and the water's heritage. Most probably it is the unique configurations of the so-called molecular clusters that enable water to store information. This facility might help explain why mineral springs possess healing qualities: their waters percolate from the earth after thousands of years of "ripening." It has been observed that when groups of sick people bathe in such waters, the bacteria does not multiply as would be expected. One person who has investigated this phenomenon is now living in Switzerland, the American chemist and water expert Joan Davis. She states: "Laboratory studies of various springs at

Baréges in France reveal a significantly slower growth rate of bacteria. Investigations on this phenomenon have revealed that it cannot be explained by material factors alone."

Esoteric attempts to "enlighten" water with words are said to succeed on a regular basis. The number of doctors who have witnessed and learned to administer water's healing gifts is growing, a development that brings them together with the shamans of indigenous peoples. Still, within the scientific community proper, the news of water's spiritual properties has awakened almost no investigative zeal.

Two scientists who did publish a work investigating water's interaction with people are the Italians A. Ansaloni and P. Vecchi. The experiment they performed in 1986 used water prepared with gold chloride, a substance that builds colloids. The two scientists reasoned that, because colloid structures influence water's coloring, they would be able to distinguish changes in energy states. The test candidates they examined fell into two groupings: "normal" people and those said to be healers.

The moment a healer placed his or her hands around a glass of tap water (without touching the glass), the color of the water changed in hue from red to blue. Likewise attempts with nonhealers seldom displayed the same phenomenon. Once such a transmutation occurred, it remained discernible even after the water was extremely diluted (>10-30). The men could only conclude that water must have some means of assembling information and passing it along. Upon subjecting the water samples used in the experiment to a resonance spectrum analysis, Ansaloni and Vecchi observed that the greatest fluctuations occurred in the zone between 7 to 10 Hertz—the area most particularly relevant to living processes.

In another experiment, samples of spring water and tap water were strongly diluted with distilled water (a relationship of 1:10 ^{50}). From a chemist's standpoint, the two water samples were identical. Yet, once gold chloride was mixed with the water, the variation of color between the two samples was dramatic.

The results of the experiments made by the two Italians have often been verified: Spectrum analyses in the infrared areas repeatedly reveal fluctuating degrees of absorption at lower frequencies. In Zurich in 1991, an experiment was performed using water flowing through a hose situated within a magnetic field. The water was measured before and after its treatment by a core resonance spectroscope, measurements that revealed marked changes. Although this experiment could evidence no "long-term memory" on the part of water, it did show that, at least in the short-term, the water "remembered" its magnetic handling.

Water surprises: It turns to steam at 212° Fahrenheit (instead of at -148° Fahrenheit, the temperature one would presume after comparing related molecular structures), and freezes at 32° Fahrenheit (instead of at -184° Fahrenheit). Water steams and thaws at temperature points threefold warmer than reason would tell us. Joan Davis notes, "We must recognize that there would be no *normal* life on earth if water behaved as we think of as *normal*."

The geologist James Hutton (1725–1797) was the first to compare the water circulation of the earth with the blood circulation of a human being. Most biological systems are composed primarily of water, and so the idea readily proffers itself that water is the most essential and vital element within the biosphere. During the second month of pregnancy a human fetus is composed nearly entirely of water; even when aged, the human body is made up of 60 percent water. Therefore, it is not a far-flung approximation to say that, in order to bolster the healthy state of the body and to aid its regeneration, water is as important as blood.

During the 1930s, Viktor Schauberger (nicknamed the "Water Magician"), an Austrian researcher and water theorist, also envisioned the biosphere as a living organism with water as its "lifeblood." He called the rivers, brooks, and underworld waterways the earth's network of arteries and capillaries. According to Schauberger, water was much more than the bundle of molecules described by the formula H_2O. He chose to call water the "first-born" of our universe's organic living substances. Schauberger spoke of water as a living organism requiring blood in order to metabolize effectively, sound environs. Living water, he wrote, must be afforded three fundamental rights: the liberty to travel in waves and vortexes; protection from light, heat, and high pressure; and, in order to auger the processes of diffusion, the freedom to frequent with oxygen and other atmospheric gasses.

Water has nearly been destroyed by modern, human lifestyles. Heavy metals, pesticides, chemical poisons, nuclides and, not least of all, the core condensations of airplanes, violate water's living space. Poisons that rained down from the sky some twenty years ago can now be found at depths in the earth ranging beyond 3,280 feet. Even if all those technologies infringing on water's living space were to be shut down immediately—every technology laying waste to the environment at this time—the earth's water resources would remain highly contaminated at least until the year 2050. Slowly, the earth's populace is feeling the consequences of water's waning health—water gives as it receives.

The water treatment plants piping water into our homes remove only the contaminants; the water's memory of the contaminants, its heritage, runs from our taps unfiltered. Although an analysis of drinking water might show that it is chemically pure, it is still contaminated by the memory of impurities. Disturbed electromagnetic oscillations are still resident in the water, marking it. This hidden aspect—an immensely important one for our health—is not considered in any of our water quality analyses. The high potentials (extreme dilutions) homeopathic medicine employs work not through the presence of substances, but through the information passed along by

infinitesimal amounts. Keeping this in mind, what can we do but gnash our teeth when we consider that, as it flows through Germany, the waters of the Rhine, waters that have been drunk and discharged by thousands of people, water that has been condensed at two or three nuclear power plants, water that has passed through the sluiceways of four or five chemical plants, arrives at the Netherlands border to be "purified" into fresh drinking water.

Much in the tradition of Viktor Schauberger, Johann Grander, an Austrian researcher and inventor, is trying to revitalize our dead-energy, badly abused waters—you might say that Grander is attempting to "heal" our water. Though a process of self-regeneration, the water he treats "lives" once more. Grander's "magnetic motor" marks the beginning of a new wave of water theory. In his motor or generator, specially paired magnets are circuited so that a state of reciprocal excitement builds. Natural magnetic forces are amplified so that energy begins to flow. The result is a potent form of natural energy that is not only patently safe but highly efficient (not compromised by heat loss). The magnetic vibrations thrown off by his motor is the energy that revitalizes the water. High-vibration water, or "Living Water," as it is sometimes called, possesses original and inherited information of the highest quality. Gardeners who use Grander's Living Water unanimously attest to the marked improvements in health and vigor among their plants and vegetables. In China, water-energizers based on Grander's theories have been installed on many diesel locomotives. Wrapped as a mantel covering around the diesel piping, the water-energizers are said to intensify diesel combustion and to occasion less exhaust. Johann Grander received a certificate from the Chinese in which he was called, "The Century's Most Important Inventor." Western scientists, however, remain overwhelmingly skeptical. The Bavarian Sabine Brückmann, a biologist and water question resource person, believes that new scientific directions must be pursued: "The questions we ask as scientists are determined by the studies we have behind us. In order to examine new phenomena we have to come up with new questions. What we find here are answers waiting for the right questions."

Water is sacred, the indigenous people tell us. What is it that we hold sacred? Jerry Mander, an American critic of technology, wrote a book in 1991 entitled *In the Absence of the Sacred*. Mander argues that the reason we plunder our planet of its resources with such unquenchable greed is that we no longer value anything as sacred. Dying to live up to its advertising, our civilization turns the earth's resources into products mirroring our inner vacuity.

Gold is one such product. Formerly, gold—based on an economic agreement—wandered from earth to treasury safe. But today, a new gold rush has begun—one fueled by fashion. According to a report issued by the World Watch Institute in June of 1993, 85 percent of the gold resources mined from the earth—some 2,550 tons annually—is manufactured into jewelry. Around the globe, the Earth's veins of gold are being slit open—in the meantime some sixty-nine countries have joined in the leaching. State-of-the-art technologies have made the new gold boom possible, technologies that can turn even the slenderest of finds into a profit. What this can mean is that per gram of gold extracted from the earth, up to 999,999 grams of pulverized rock remain behind—that adds up to some twenty tons for a ring! Commonly, because it binds to the fine gold particles, a solution of cyanide is poured over the gold-bearing rock. As a substitute for cyanide, the hordes of gold-diggers who each day press further into the Amazon rain forests use mercury. Not only do these fortune hunters hazard their own lives, but they contaminate the earth and ground water of Brazil's virgin lands.

Cyanide is a salt derived from (highly toxic) prussic acid. Precautionary measures practiced at gold-milling sites are never in keeping with the posed environmental jeopardy. In the tropics, whether it's because the gold-bearing rock is treated with cyanide in leaky containers, or whether it's because heavy rains flood the leaching ponds, or whether it's because contaminated poisons seep past haphazardly built security levies, polluted water and dead fish mark the sites of almost every gold operation. For each gram of gold, as much as 6 feet of water is directly contaminated. The average lifetime of such upstart gold-mining operations is ten years. What such operations leave in their wakes are destroyed farmlands and severely contaminated water tables—areas no longer habitable. The same story repeats itself all over the globe. Usually—be it the Yanomami of the Amazon, the Western Shoshone of Nevada, or the Ubo of the Philippines—it is the indigenous peoples who are forced from the lands.

Gold versus water. The end of our century, our millennium, will be marked by a spiraling wave of conflicts and court battles between the destroyers and the protectors of water. Not only cyanide and mercury, but acid rain and chemicals such as chlorine, contaminate the world's water resources daily. Chlorine gas was employed in warfare during World War I; owing to its hideous effects on the human respiratory system, it was eventually outlawed by the Geneva Convention. Since the 1930s, chlorine has been used in the production of solvents, weed pesticides, plastics, varnishes, and paints. Chlorine bleaches paper and decalcifies water. Over 40 million tons of chlorine are used annually throughout the world. Chlorine is cheap to manufacture.

But a cheap chemical can exact a heavy mortgage. Because organic chlorine products are not to be found in nature, the immune systems of fauna and flora are routed. Chlorine, a lasting environmental pollutant, the antithesis of "biodegradable," has taken up residence in our food chain. In the meantime chlorine can be found most everywhere: in water supplies, in rain, in glaciers—traces have even been found in Antarctica's remotest stretches of ice. Chlorinated chemicals have been linked to cancer and genetic mutation. Because only nonsoluble substances that can be scraped from active carbon filters are eligible for scientific study, the dangers arising from a number of chlorinated chemicals defy analysis. Chlorine has been shown to damage the heart's mitral valve and to inhibit the ability of red blood cells to carry oxygen. Yet most communities use chlorine to treat their water supplies and make their drinking water *safe*.

Our waterworks cry out for new models. The process of pumping and storing water employed today by modern water treatment plants serve only to weaken water's vigor and character. Centrifugal movements under high pressure exact a toll analogous to what can happen within our blood systems: Like a case of creeping arteriosclerosis, ionized water particles under pressure sludge the walls of water pipes to crystallize into hard crusts. Analyses of healthy drinking water found at hundreds of mountain springs record mineral residues. At an earlier time, when wooden piping was used, these minerals remained intact in the water. Cities now lay galvanized steel pipes, piping that not only strips water of its electrical properties, but also rapes it of minerals—those very elements that could contribute to the healthy regeneration of our bodies. The fate of the mega cities is written beneath their streets.

There are some cities famous for their water. The water that pours from the faucets of Munich, for example, is better in quality than most expensive bottled mineral waters. But let's trace the water back from the faucets of Munich to its source. The spring beneath Marienplatz at the center of Munich is, like all the springs within the city's borders, drinkable only at risk to health. The people of Munich drink water from the Alps, water piped in from the Mangfalltal and from the Loisach. During the Middle Ages, a person who siphoned off the water of others was hung by his feet in a well.

•

The fact of water's worldwide mishandling and mistreatment presses a single question forward. Namely, how will it all end? It is as if a man starts a ball down a slope and a spectator steps forward to ask whether the ball will ever arrive at the bottom. The answer: if no one stops it, it's doomed to. We can use the same answer here. In order to guarantee the coming generations' healthy water, we must change our ways. What the new way will look like and how it will fall into place and where it will lead cannot yet be answered. The sole certainty is that the present way is false.

Tatanka Yotake, the famous medicine man of the Hunkpapa-Lakota, the man the Whites called Sitting Bull, once said: "When a man loses something, he will turn around and go back and look for it before he continues along his way." The relationship with nature we have lost cannot simply be replaced by something kicked up from the side of the path. Much more searching is needed before we can find an honest way to restore to health our relationship with ourselves and with nature. A few legal scholars, much in the tradition of the Maori, have risen up to defend nature and to grant it a voice— perhaps this marks a beginning. One pioneer of the environmental rights movement is the American Legal Professor Christopher D. Stone. His provocative book, *Should Trees Have Standing?* poses the question: Why should a mountain or a lake or a forest or an animal species not have the right to be represented by lawyers in a court of law, when a firm—clearly no living entity—is granted such right? Legally, land, flora, and fauna are yet treated as possessions.

Stone demands not only that such entities have the right to act as plaintiffs, but that nature be accorded a fundamental standing unmitigated by human values, that natural entities should be accorded a set of intrinsic and inalienable rights regardless of utility or beauty.

A river that burns should be able to sue.

ACKNOWLEDGMENTS

I would like to thank everyone at Frederking & Thaler Verlag in Germany for all their inspiration and good partnership in originating this book and so many others. I am especially indebted to Christian Frederking and of course to Monika Thaler, whose tireless efforts matched with grace, kindness and thoughtfulness have made so many good things happen for me. I would like to thank everyone at Stewart Tabori & Chang, and especially Lena Tabori and Jennifer Walsh, for having the faith and the drive to bring this book to the English-speaking world.

Finally, I would like to thank my coworkers Mel Calvin, Heather Donlan, Christine Eckhoff, Ray Pfortner, Craig Scheak, Deirdre Skillman, and Lisa Woods. Together they always ensure that things flow smoothly the many months each year that I am away shooting. Their teamwork and commitment make books like this one possible at all.

A.W.

Published in 1999 and distributed in the U.S. by
Stewart, Tabori & Chang,
a division of U.S. Media Holdings, Inc.
115 West 18th Street, New York, NY 10011

Designed by Melanie Random

First published in German by
© 1997 Frederking & Thaler Verlag, Munich,
a division of Verlagsgruppe Bertelsmann GmbH
Photos © Art Wolfe
Text © Michelle Gilders, Claus Biegert
Original title: *Wasser. Welten zwischen Himmel und Erde*

Library of Congress Catalog Card Number: 98-86718

Printed in Italy

10 9 8 7 6 5 4 3 2 1